# Daniel's Story

# By Antoine Larosiliere

First paperback edition September 2019

ISNN  9781081830045

Published by Kindle Direct Publishing a subsidiary of Amazon

# MEET MAMA BULLY

## Chapter 1

In case you were wondering, I'm still in my tiny
twin bed.
5:00 a.m. on my Iron Man alarm clock, it read.
Wide awake, nervous, with all kinds of
thoughts in my head,
Bed springs and metal things poking me,
I'll sleep better when I'm dead...
I see a rat and some roaches in the corner
playing "keep away" with some bread.
One roach threw it like a football, and the
other, with his tiny roach legs, sped
With the rat in the middle, ready to tackle
who fled.

I'm also looking at the new clothes I chose on the chair that I spread.

Through the darkness, my vision's sharpness, straight infrared.

New jeans, t-shirt, and a blue Yankee cap with a brim that's red.

I imagined, "Who's that fly new kid?" are the words that will be said.

Walking through the hallway as if there's a soundtrack playing and by the beat I'm being led.

The girls looking at me like I'm what they hope to wed.

All the fellas showing me love as if I have some fictitious street cred.

Been planning this outfit for weeks since I dread

What my Mama would choose would have me looking like a first-class loser instead.


First day at a new school isn't the only reason I'm up; truth is,

I could still smell the old pee scent that lingers on my mattress.

Peed in the bed till I was eight years old,
but wearing grown up diapers was the saddest.

Mama threatening to bring my pee-stained
bedding to school made me the maddest.

I can hear sirens outside my window.
And the neighborhood wino, arguing with our
building's widow.
He relieved himself behind the building, but
here's the issue....

He wiped himself with her Balinese cat
instead of tissue.

I can hear Mama yelling at Pops every morning,
the way she do.
Calling him a "retard" calling him an "idiot" all he
ever says is, "Yeah, you too!"
Argues with him, "Good for nothing, that's why
we're always struggling; I wish I wasn't
married to you."
He says, "I'm the only one who can deal with
you—
Woman let me be, I leave for work in a few."

Oh, by the way, I share a room with my
annoying sister.
She's over there drooling on her pillow, making
it smell bitter.
She makes me watch all these girly shows; it
blows when I'm with her.
When no one's home and things go wrong,
she blames me; so, I rather a sitter.

She's only two years older, but it feels like 10;
Because she acts like she's my mother.
One time, I was in a fight and she got between
us, so, I lost another.

She even goes around bragging about how she chipped my tooth.
It was an accident from both of us pulling on an elastic belt, but I ain't got no proof.

She calls me names I hate, then laughs while she does a shimmy.
Instead of awkward, she calls me doofus; and calls me bony because I'm skinny.
And every time I mess up, she says I'm the chairperson of some loser committee.
Sometimes she acts just like Mama, so to me she's Mama's mini.

It's 6:30 now, time to get up and let this first day begin.
Brushed my teeth, took a shower, when I got out, fresh new wears were missing.

Asked Mama, "Where did it go?"
She said she took them. "Dadi, I'm not raising you to be no brute!"
She pulled out what I thought she threw out, an official dork Super Suit!

Bowtie, briefcase, and shirt made in Jamaica.

And some Michael Jackson penny loafers;
boy, I really hate her.

And by the way, what's the deal with the
briefcase?
She must think I have a part time job
working in an office space.
And those penny loafers, shoes without a
lace.
With a slit for money, like I can't be poor
with grace.
And if I'm running from a dog or in some kind
of race,
Not only will I look stupid, but I'll slip and
fall flat on my face.

I couldn't say no, I had no choice, my mom's
a tyrant.
She makes Hitler seem like Ghandi,
and the Incredible Hulk appear non-violent.
She wore a permanent frown, eyebrows
down, with a back like Brock Lesnar.
With her Haitian accent, she even spoke
aggressively like a wrestler.

In middle school and high school, Mama was a thug who would beat up her brother's bullies and their parents, too.
Tainted and spray-painted their pets in blue, Intimidated and threatened everyone she knew.

Pops never tried to fight, except that one
time he chased away a car crook.
He didn't like to argue, and many insults he
took.
He always wore a smile; he had that "nice
guy" look.
He wasn't very tall; he could probably fit in
Mama's pocket book.
He wasn't very handy; always calling the
super, Mr. Sam Snook.
He hated cleaning, he would ask me and my
sister to get him off the hook.
Hard-boiled eggs are the only thing he could
cook.
And snakes, spiders and lizards, always had
him shook.

While Mama was beating up bullies in school,
Pops was running and fear was his stench.
And one time, the cops found Pops hiding
after school underneath a park bench.

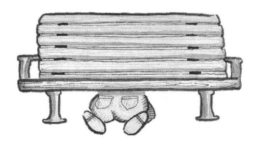

Oh, I almost forgot, I don't want you to get too confused.
My name is Daniel, but that's not the name Mama just used.
Every Haitian has a nickname that's given, even if you refuse.
You can try and not respond to it, but it's a battle you'll always lose.
Most of the Haitian nicknames make no sense.
It's a way of showing love, but who wants their two cents?
I'm called Dadi, even though I'm no one's daddy, and this is where it will commence.
To call someone "Ti Dodo" meaning "Little Sleep" you gotta be dense.
How you get "Poushon" from the name Ralf, and "Dadou" from Andre has no defense.
Some other nicknames, when translated to English, I could understand if someone considered it as an offense.
How can you call someone with the names Domonique "Ti Doodoo," and Carline "Ti Caca", meaning "Small Turd", at their expense?
My aunt Esther is "Ti Tete" which means "Little Breast"; but hers are immense.
My cousin Stephany is called "Fany" even though her butt is as flat as a picket fence.

15

As you can see, most Haitian nicknames end in -i for the long /e/ sound or -ou for the long /oo/ sound, hence:
Louis is "Loulou", Michele is "Michou", and Patricia is "Patoutou".
Ginette is "Gigi", Najami is "Mimi", and there's my uncle "FanFan", too.
If you haven't noticed, alliteration is a big part of what we do, so we condense and turn Joanne into "Jojo", and Joyceleen into "Joujou".
Sometimes your nickname is based on what's wrong with you;
Have an uncle who calls me "Ti Mouye" (Little Wet), since I pee in the bed— I hate that it's true.


So, I put on the Dork Super Suit, but I also packed a change of clothes.
Stuffed it in my briefcase and made sure that it stayed closed.
When Mama asked, "Why is your bag so full?" I swear, I almost froze.
Said, "It's school supplies;" was so scared, I blew a nervous fart right by her nose.

Went to the kitchen to grab some breakfast
and leave.

I open up my Cheerios box, I see things you
wouldn't believe!

Poured some cereal in my bowl...there it goes!

A roach is hula-hooping with my Cheerios.

One had an obstacle course going,

One was in my milk floating,

One was seeing how long he could hold onto
the Cheerio when it rolls.

One used it as a steering wheel, as if driving
a speedboat, while standing on its tippy toes.

A couple used it as a basketball hoop,
shooting jump shots through the holes.

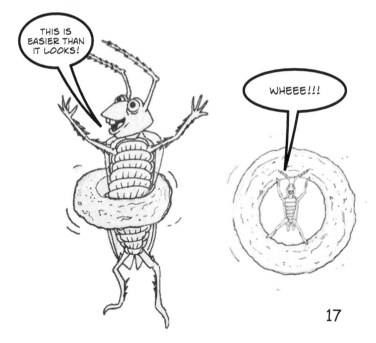

17

Looked to see what Mama packed me for
lunch; just another thing kids will tease.
Instead of a sandwich like other mothers do,
she always packs me rice and peas.
Or, some thick Haitian bread, so hard you
couldn't squeeze.
Inside it is some extra thick, certified,
government cheese,
with butter instead of mayo, to choke to
death—but no guarantees.

It was almost time to go, grabbed my
favorite sneakers before Mama can see.
But you know she got that x-ray vision,
so, of course she caught me.
I said, "I might have gym today." She gave a
look like I'm a dummy.
She said, "You have other sneakers, why
grab the ones that smell funny?"

When the bus came, ran down the squeaky
steps, as if running from a brawl.
Passed the elevator that's always broken,
with graffiti on the wall.
It still smelled like bum piss, that was worse
than a bathroom stall.

Two midsize men were smoking in the lobby,
and though they were small,
the cloud of smoke almost made me choke,
and it stood almost 10-feet tall.
As I approached the bus, jokes and names you
can hear the kids call.
Went through the bus door, and up the bus
steps, trying not to fall.
The next thing I know— got hit in the face
with a paper ball.

# Meet the Bus Bullies

## Chapter 2

After the paper ball to the face, and
another to the side of the head,
First thing I saw was the bus driver's— face,
his eyes bloodshot red.
Next thing I noticed, he had a stutter
and he tried to say something.
It was G...G...G...Goo...Goo...Goo...Good
Mo...Mo...Morning.

He was dressed like the '70s; teeth rotten
from cavities,
As if eating junk was one of his specialties.
He must have ran out the house without
brushing, because he hurries?
Hair slicked back, bald spot, listening to old
school melodies.
Kept looking back like he wanted to commit
felonies.
He had that "I can't stand you kids" facial
disease.
Tray full of candies, yelling at the kids with
a case of the fidgeties...

Walking through this storm of paper balls
is a treacherous feat.
Two boys in the front playing with trading
cards,
snorting and ignoring the garbage at their
feet.
Trying to be discrete,
one had a homemade haircut that was
obviously incomplete.
Wearing throwback sneakers, that are so
far back, they're obsolete.
The other had on a fake baseball cap—
hope his mother kept the receipt.
It's like they took my life and put it on
repeat.
It's like their mothers and my Mama had
traded secrets after a meet and greet.
But at least they don't have on a Dork
Super Suit, looking like a geek.
I can feel the collision of the butterflies
inside me peak.
More nervous than an innocent man sitting
in a cop car, handcuffed in the backseat.
Everyone staring, some probably thinking,
"Oh look, fresh meat."
Then I put a little bop in my walk, to
disguise the fact that I want to retreat.

Bus engine idling like it's about to overheat.
And you can smell the garbage from outside,
and its stench on the street .

Passed two more boys in the front sitting
side- by-side.
One sitting with his back stiff, hoping he
wasn't on this bus ride,
or like he just cried.
Fidgeting, no kidding, like to a judge he just
lied.

The one to the left,
was eating till out of breath.
Talking to himself about which snack is best,
while crumbs landing on his chest, decorating
his vest.

Doritos, Cheetos, a Honeybun, some of the
things he was pushing
Into his mouth, when a piece fell out, he even
licked the seat cushion.

In the middle rows you had the girls who
chose to listen to music.
On their phones, they play every song, so
everyone can hear it.

They sang along, but sounded wrong, like a
bad karaoke trick.
The boys weren't any better, having a
session of lousy hip-hop.
One was on the beat box, then banged on
the seat tops.
Two freestyle battle while the beat drops.

The beat box is mostly spitting.
The freestyle made no sense,
Who's "slapping kittens with mittens"?
And the other's verse is even worse;
He cursed and spoke about fried chicken.
And also said, "Keep my sister's name out
your mouth." But the reason why, he's
omitting.

There's this one boy— for now let's just call
him "Pretty Boy Shawn."
Like mosquitoes to water, girls to him seem
drawn.
He puts his arms around them, plays with
their hair, like an act he puts on.
If that was any other boy, these girls would
be gone.

If that was me, they'd probably disinfect the seat with a baby wipe.
Maybe walk away and say "sike."
Tell me to get lost or even take a hike.
Maybe for not being cool enough or the right height.
Or some kind of zebra without the white stripe.
Wish I was a fly guy, or someone's type.
One day I hope to know what being "Pretty Boy Shawn" feels like.


One kid hung out the window insulting people as they walked by...
First he says "Hi" and if there's no reply—
He commences with the dissing and then he says "goodbye."
He didn't discriminate, he harassed every girl and guy.
I'm surprised his head fit, because his neck was thick as a thigh.
His nose is dripping everywhere, no lie.
He had the nerve to throw at people a half-eaten french fry.
They should have thrown something back and hit him in the eye.

Or with his head out there, bird poop should
fall out the sky.
Some kids laughed, just to laugh, no matter
if the jokes were dry.
They might be just as scared as I am, so
instead they decide to comply.
I avoided eye contact with him, as if I'm just
too shy.
My outfit alone is begging for attention, and
I hope he doesn't reply.

He says to Jose, "Is that your cousin?
"Am I seeing what I'm seeing, or am I
bugging?
Did he eat one donut or the whole dozen?
That must be why his shirt wouldn't button."

He says to Lisa "There goes your uncle,
With his big old nose,
Sucking in our clothes
Through his nostrils."

He says to Kenny, "Is that your sister?
Is she a Miss or Mister?
You shake her hand, or do you kiss her?
But I'm not trying to diss her."

There's this one kid, it seems his goal was to disgust.
He keeps yelling out "deez nuts"
from the back of the bus.
Flipping his eyelids, making girls cuss,
squeezing his pimples till they bust,
and showing the puss.
Making armpit farting noises,
he thinks it's a must.
And spitting spitballs in the girls' hair,
made a big fuss.

Tried to sit next to this one kid in a seat
that looked like it was pecked at by a bird.
But he placed his book bag there, implying
that it's reserved.
As if I'm not just a geek or a nerd.
But more like the world's biggest human
turd.
Next, I tried to sit next to this girl, although
it wasn't preferred.
As soon as she saw me, she purposely laid
across both seats, and I'm thinking *that
couldn't have just occurred.*
I even tried to say "*Excuse me,*" but she
pretended like nothing was heard.

This other girl said the seat was broken, the same seat she was sitting in...say word?
Did you hear that load of crap she just served?
Even Rosa Parks, I'm sure, would say that this is absurd.

I eventually took an empty seat next to a boy sleeping,
so I sat there real quiet.
Then this big kid was stalking the aisle, who said he had tried about three diets.

Diet one— must be for the tire that he had wrapped around his waist.
Diet two— could be for his man boobs that he smears on the window in the passenger's face.
Diet three— is likely for his triple chin action that's flapping all over the place.

He was slapping kids in the back of the head and playing drums on some of the others.
He laughed and went to join two boys who were cracking jokes on people's mothers.

Saying, "Your mother is so fat," and "Your mother is so small.
Your mother is so dumb," but they weren't funny at all.

I wanted to say, *You're fat!*
I wanted to say, *You're dumb!*
I wanted to say, *Go back to licking jelly doughnut crumbs!*
You're probably wondering, where is this coming from?
But I see these victims, afraid that's what I'll become.
But for now, I'll sit here wishing he sits on some gum.
And don't make a sound, not a whisper or even a hum.

One of the girls called this bus bully "Hank, Hank Blaylock."
He had a scent that could empty out a parking lot.
He had a mohawk,
And someone even called him pork chop.
He kept some snacks in a fanny pack and ziplock.
Ankle fat kept pushing down his gym sock,
And a big belly made his jersey shirt crop.

# Hank the Stank

The girls complained about a smell
and who to accuse.
Said the bus was smelling like two pet zoos.
Not sure if it was my gym shoes,
or the sweat from Hank's ginormous man
boobs.
Or the kid next to me, farting in his sleep—
Either way, I consider it a lose-lose.

There are flies flying through the funk fog.
At one point they're sprinting, then doing a
light jog.
Maybe they think there's a sewer backed up,
or toilet clogged.

They're going in circles; maybe they're trying
to escape the scent.
They smell with their antennas, right now
they're likely all bent.

Trying to keep my eyes on them, sometimes don't know where they went.
They're probably all spent.
Some windows are open, but the force of the wind probably feels like a wall of cement.
That's hard for them to penetrate or make a dent.
Maybe all of this buzzing is them having an argument
About whether they should go through the window or squeeze through the air vent.

As the girls are playing and singing their songs,
Wish I had a phone to distract me from everything that's going on.
When I ask Mama, she says the payphone isn't broken, which is usually wrong.
Who uses a payphone these days, they're so filthy, you need to use prongs.
Dying to get off the bus, hope it won't be too long.
Just got hit with a spitball from the kid with the pimples who's looking real strong.
Looking real grown, *in what grade does he belong?*

I would do something, if I wasn't the size of
Jane
and he wasn't the size of King Kong.

I'm watching this other kid in a jumpsuit
who's been dancing for the past mile.
Hair smeared on his forehead emo-style.
He had the thinnest lips with teeth he needs
to file
That looked like pieces of broken bathroom
tiles.
His nose was spread and he had a buck-tooth
smile.
On each one of his shoulders was a pile
Of volcanic ash that left a trail as long as
the Nile.
He would pop-lock in the middle of the aisle,
Then stop and rock in his seat for a while.

*Why is the window fool scowling at the dancing kid for goodness sake?*
*It's as if he's wishing and praying that his legs would break.*

Maybe he can't dance, even to a song by Drake.

This bus is filled with haters, make no mistake.

Dancing is something I guess Hank also can't take.

So, he shoved the dancing kid like a poisonous snake.

And falling from this kid's hair, I see snowflakes.


The bus engine sounds like a growl from an angry troll.

It's shaking, and I feel the vibrations from the windows to the console.

There is a smell of wet dog and plastic, that is dirty and old;

With butt cheek stains and junk food remains that left plenty of mold.

*Oh man, what is that? Did we just hit a speed bump or a pothole?*

Some celebrate like it's the first day of parole.

Whoa! Now he stopped short and turned as if
avoiding a pole.
Everyone is trying to grab onto something
they can hold.
Some girls seemed scared— if they were
acting, then I was sold.
The screams and cheers we couldn't control.
And anticipation of the next bump was taking
its toll.
It felt like something just gave a sudden jolt
to my soul.
Like inside my pants someone placed hot coal.
Even the Spanish kids would curse in Español.
The boys ramming their heads, as if
exaggerating the impact is the goal.
Saw the dancing kid fly down the aisle, as he
did a tootsie roll.
Even Hank took a break from his usual stroll,
Because he dropped, then flopped like some
jelly in a bowl.
It was as if the boy's cool pose someone or
something stole?
The jerks did things that hurt and continued
their role.
Like, purposely landing on some poor chump
and squeezing his mole.

A voyage to misery this bus driver led.
Not wishing for a bus crash, but prayed to
God he sped.
Hank saw my sleeping buddy
knocked like he took some meds.
He just laid there as if he was dead.
Or, like he was home in his own bed.
The hair hanging over his eyebrow Hank
spread.
Grabbed a marker and wrote something
on his forehead.


Confused and upset at what I read,
"I suc," instead of "I suck," is what it said.
Hank can't spell, not even a shred.
So it's not just food, but also on self-esteem
he's fed...
Wish I could nudge him, and wake him, but
lightly I tread;
It was only in my mind I pled.
Tried to ignore this prank kid's dread,
So he doesn't turn the attention to me
instead.
He kept lurking, my nerves had my face
flushed red.
Sweating to the point of a couple of pounds I
shed.

He was intimidating, as if a Sumo
wrestler and a rhinoceros were bred.
Then he said, "Wait!" right before he
fled.

And he looked at me and called me,
" 'Prince of Dorkness.'
You must be president of the club,
'Dorks Anonymous.'
Why don't you tell us how real
dork life is?
You look a little sick...
Are you suffering from 'Dork-itis?'

Where did u get those clothes?
Was there a sale at 'Dork-Mart?'
That smell must be your sneakers,
or did you release a 'dork fart?'

What is your nationality?
Are you a 'Dork-arean?'
Why are there so many of you?
Is it 'dork season?' "

# MY TEACHER IS A BULLY

## Chapter 3

Woke up the kid next to me, and asked, "Are you ok?"

Don't sleep on the bus. Then showed him a pic with his own phone of the price he had to pay.

We arrived at school with no delay.

Rushed off the bus in a pushing and shoving melee.

Passed the bus driver with a mouth full of decay.

Eyes rolled back in his head like a seizure was on its way.

I had an idea of what he was trying to say.

He got stuck on the /g/ from "Have a g-g-good day!"

In front of the school, before we go in, just a couple of things to point out.

There's this one kid, embarrassed, head like a brussel sprout.

To go inside, he took the quickest route.

His dad's car was beat up,
and when he pulled up,
all you heard was put-put-put.
Paint job was camouflage as smoke filled the
street.
Tires wobbly, rims bent, and bumper scraping
against the concrete.

There's this other kid, who grabbed a hold of
the flagpole
exposing his belly button that looked like a
spring roll,

and his SpongeBob underwear that was blue
and yellow.
He is wearing a W.W.E. t-shirt that was retro.
His stomach wiggled and giggled like wet dough.
His mother pulling on his elbow, hoping he'd let
go.
Her voice so sharp, you can hear it echo.
But he just kept cursing and said, "No!"
The only thing that worked is when she
offered him Jell-o.
She had a pack in her purse, she should've
offered it from the get-go.
And you can tell, well, he and his mother are
special.

Once inside, the hallway is packed with people.

So many morons in one place can't be legal.

There are dorks, losers, and geeks,

Airheads and freaks.

There are fake tough guys, fake superstars and idiots.

Outcasts, weirdos and them stuck-up chicks;

I see wannabes and bullies;

Punks, thugs and woosies.

There goes the athletes and ballers,

Fly guys and brawlers;

Class clowns and those emo kids.

Floors newly waxed so I almost slid.

It was bright like the light bulbs had no lid.

Fresh coat of paint on the walls to rid,

The graffiti and memories from the year before they hid.

To keep us from hanging in the hallway, it was extra frigid.

Put my head down, looked around for my class- is what I did.


Went from wrong door to wrong door;

from 153 to 144.

Then got shoved to the floor by two dinosaurs.

One had a big head, short arms, and pecs
like a T-Rex.
The other is skinny like a raptor; long neck,
small head, and teeth like daggers.

Here comes the school security guard;
Running his mouth and checking I.D. cards.
His name tag said Solomon, but someone
called him Mr. Charles.
He had dreads, maybe a couple of yards,
Thick enough to pull cars.
His teeth were like prisoners serving life
behind bars.
He reeked of cheap cologne, and old man
cigars.
He said he walks with a limp, because one of
his legs retards.
Instead of saying "excuse me," he just says,
"pards."

# "Sarge"

He said he spent time in the military—
sometimes he's referred to as, "Sarge."
He spoke of conspiracies, and how "The
Man's" in charge.
While his mustache flaps, and it's quite bushy
and large.
He interrupts our explanations with blatant
disregard.
With no hesitation, into any conversation he'll
barge.

When he walks, he staggers.
Wearing a wrinkled uniform, his saggy pants
he gathers.
Got in between me, the T-Rex, and the
raptor,
Like he had a dinosaur tracker.
He called us all a bunch of slackers.

40

Then told these two dinosaurs, to go do
something that matters.

Picked myself up, and resumed looking for my
classroom.
When I finally found it, suddenly consumed
with the feeling of doom.
Walked in, and then 20 eyes on me went—
zoom!
Felt the fear and failure of students past in
this tomb.
This must be my teacher— she said, "Hello,
I'm Mrs. Vanswoon."
Behind her fake smile, you can see a snarl
loom;
As if on her wedding day, she murdered her
groom.
Half of her face sags, like a deflated balloon;
As if when she slept, that half was left out
of the cocoon.
Is that her real face, her real clothes, or a
witch's costume?
That's how she must have got to work, I
assume;
Because, in the corner there's a dustpan and
broom.

Vicks and mothballs are the smells of her perfume.
I wonder if she mutates into something else at the sight of the moon....
Does she get more evil from morning to afternoon?
She must keep a creature on a leash like a pet from a lagoon.
To holy water and crosses, I hope she's not immune.
As if she wasn't scary enough— I sense much worse is coming soon.

She stood us all up in the back of the class so she can make a seating chart.
Sitting us boy/girl, boy/girl is my least favorite part.

Set up in the shape of "U," or a horse shoe.
Sat me in between two— with some kid's back zits in view.
Also next to a girl named Jules, who seems to have a couple of loose screws;
Who kept on playing with stickers, and eating the glues.

To my right, another named Myrtle, who seems to have a thing for Marge Simpson hairdos.
She kept staring at me like I'm a brand new pair of shoes,
The way a drunk looks at a bottle of booze.
Behind me, is that pimple-faced kid who couldn't wait to take a snooze.

The walls are decorated with plain views,
Like the prison walls you see on the news.
Felt like I'm in for a long year of being abused;
As if I didn't pay enough grammar school dues..
It's like I was about to be interrogated for something I'm accused;
Or waiting for a beatdown, or an ego bruise.
I wish there was a way we could choose,
but this witch would hex me if I refuse.
I decided to ask anyway. She said, "It's a dictatorship, I say and you do."
But last time I checked, dictators are bullies, too.

My sister had told me that middle school and high school is all a big game.

Now I'm pretty smart, but if my grades show that, then I'm considered a lame.

To be on the Honor Roll and to roll with honor and dignity just ain't the same.

I don't wanna grow old, telling a room full of cats about the loser I became.

Some people are here to learn, and others are here to make a name.

You can do it with sports, clothes, jokes, or being a tough guy who can inflict pain.

If your clothes are always fly, that's the quickest way to fame.

For me, it won't be clothes; to look like a baby Barack Obama is Mama's aim.

If you choose sports, you gotta practice all the time like you're insane.

But, if you still suck, there'll be a pic of you in the locker room's wall of shame.

Plus, I can't be a tough guy; you've seen my Urkel-like frame.

If you try to be the funny guy— when things go wrong, you get all the blame.

I'll have to practice cracking jokes inside my mind, before I stake my claim.

Once we all sat down, we went through some classroom rules.
But, there's a couple that's trouble, or perhaps made for fools.

## "Follow directions the first time."
*What? We can't get a do-over?*
*What if I was daydreaming, or hard of hearing, or need to sit closer?*

## "Raise your hand before you speak."
*What if I forgot to use deodorant;*
*Underarms stinking, and the smell is intolerant?*

## "Make smart choices."
*What if I'm dumb as a tic tac, and can't do much better?*
*How about trial and error, and hope it doesn't take forever?*

## "Don't get out of your seat without permission."
*What if my butt crack starts itching, or in my pants I'm pissing?*

She began to take attendance, she called it
the "roll call."
I'm glad during this time I wasn't in the
bathroom stall.

Because the "roll call" was pure comic relief.
Out of my seat, I was about to fall.
One of the first names is Dehandsome, but
he wasn't handsome at all.

I heard names like Hennessy and Alize,
names I saw in my uncle's bar.
There was a Lexus and a Mercedes, but
neither is a luxury car.

There was an angel named Simone, that had
me in a trance, anyone can tell.
Her friend with the big butt's name was
Heaven, but she is more like hell.

There is an African kid named Mofojoles,
but told the teacher to call him "Mofo."
After that, it was hard to contain the
chatter; so, Vanswoon just told him, "No."

His brother's name is Dabaub, pronounced
"Da-Boob", even more of a disaster.

I can see it now, he'll be nicknamed "Titi-Boy;" which is pure laughter.

There is this weird girl, and her name is As-Unique.
But it should have been As-U-Reek, because she smelled like my pee-stained sheet.

She made us write down emergency contact information.
Sounds like a setup, I'm having "giving-the-wrong-number" contemplations.

What's she bugging us for? The main office should have that.
But she rather we rat on ourselves and tell her where we hide at.
I'm no fool, this is a trap.
So, she can fly to our homes in the middle of the night like a bat;
On her broomstick in a pointy black hat.
But, most of us live in the hood; where there's no welcome mat.
If she comes, hope she's ready for combat.

This is all a big joke; then I cleared my throat.

47

Asked to use the sharpener because the
point on my pencil broke.

Went to the back, by the sharpener in my
Snoop Dog pace.
The desks were close together, so I
squeezed through a tight space.
Then, someone stuck their foot out, their
sneaks had no lace.
That caused me to trip, without a pinch of
grace.
It was so sudden, for the impact, there was
no time to brace.
I landed head first against the bookcase.
And then one book after another tumbled
onto my face.

He pulled back his shin, and I looked back at
him.
Where do I begin?
He had a head like a bowling pin, eyes sunken
in, and wide like the Joker's grin.
Witch Vanswoon, with a deadly spin was
asking, "What happened?"
But I gave it away when I looked at him.
Then he stared back at me like a cold-
blooded assassin;

Or, a four-foot serial killer with a Popeye chin.

I didn't snitch, it's where my eyes took aim.
Then, witch Vanswoon realized he was to blame.
He got in trouble, so his eyes turned red with flame.
Myrtle whispered, "Mitch that wasn't funny."
So I guess that's his name.
So, this big-eyed, boxer-chin, pin-head in the class is now my newest pain.
On his way home, hope he gets hit by a train.
It might be too early, but in my mind I complained.
Because this was the worst first day the minute I came.

# cafeteria bullies

## Chapter 4

When the fourth period bell rang, I ran to
use the Men's Room,
to change into something less embarrassing
than this Dork Super Suit costume.
It was lunch time now, and if I walked in the
cafeteria dressed like this,
It would be over for me, social suicide,
straight up crisis.

So, I went in the stall, took out my clothes
shaped in a ball.
I stayed on my tippy-toes, because the stall
was pissy and small.
It is hella gross; put one leg on at a time,
hoping not to fall.
Dressed in less than five minutes, wrinkled
and all.
Looks like I slept in these clothes, and out of
bed I crawled;
Or, by Pit-Bulls and Doberman Pinchers they
were mauled.

Entered the cafeteria, and all kinds of
things are happening.
I felt like I didn't belong in this chaotic
gathering.
I sensed anything could go wrong at any
moment, and it's baffling.
Few are quiet, most were talking and
laughing
At things they heard or saw while people
were passing.
The boys are banging on the tables, using
pencils for tapping.
They're back at it, freestyling and rap
battling.
This time the topic is joke-cracking.
Like, *you're so small when you're napping;
for a bed sheet, you use a napkin.*

My fellow geeks and dorks sat close to the
entrance. Chances are, they're imagining
they're in a video game lost, or to Comic-Con
traveling.
Or, stuck in the midst of an extraterrestrial
channeling.
With Pokemon cards, they're haggling.
The athletes and fly guys were in the middle
rows thumb wrestling and grappling.

51

Also the back of each other's head, they
were slapping;
Measuring their pecks, and the pretty girls
they hassling.
The stuck up chicks and airheads sat next to
them, with lips and nails dazzling.
Trying to figure out which foods or drinks
are fattening,
Which hairstyle or outfit is more flattering.
The weirdos and emos sat in the corners,
after scattering.
Kept their head down, and said nothing; as if
words they're rationing.
Looking like being around all these jerks and
wannabes is challenging.


There are a couple of girls braiding hair,
doing nails, and gossiping,
"Who's got real hair and bra padding?
Who's bossed-up, who's cute, and who's over
there thinking she modeling?
Who's annoying, and who we dodging?
Which boys we won't mind bothering?
Who's top 5?" Over this, they're squabbling.
They continue with, "Who's looking like a
goblin?"
and "who makes us feel like vomiting?

Which boys keep looking at us while
slobbering,
and which ones stay hollering?"
Frustrations toward teachers they're also
bottling.
Saying, "What do they teach us? Not a
thing!"

Every so often, someone randomly shouts out
something embarrassing about someone else.
Like, "Keisha ain't got no boyfriend! She gave
that hickey to herself!"
"During the lock-down drill, Greg farted and
it smelled like salami,"
and "Danny accidentally called the teacher
his mommy!"
"Kelly's phone rang in class, and her ring tone
is Sir Mix A Lot's, 'Baby Got Back!' "
Someone else said, "Don't sit next to Sheila,
we saw roaches in her backpack!"

Saw the dancing kid, who can't sit still;
Dance battling two girls with real dance skills.
In the face, he was hit with tater tots in the
grill.
It bounced off his forehead as he windmills.

He is spinning on his back like the tip of a drill.
He tried to tell these boys to chill.
They still threw food at him at will.
Then, he slipped on some milk these two bullies spilled;
And he fell like he was falling down an icy hill.
With laughter the caf filled,
And it seems the kid with the snot nose is the most thrilled.
I wouldn't trade places with Flakes, not for a hundred mill.

I saw someone get hit with a plum tomato in the temple.
Someone else get smoked
with a piece of broccoli right in the throat.

I see what some do, dipping and dodging now.
One girl ducked, but it looked more like a quick bow.
With a tater tot, someone got hit in the eyebrow.
It wasn't a full blown food fight, more like a chow pow.
With a finger, some would flick veggies 10 feet in the air somehow.
None of this, did the lunch lady allow.
To get the dean every five seconds, she would threaten and vow.

She even asked us questions to probe.
Then, she got hit with a string bean on the earlobe.

Look who it is, sitting there with three lunches.
All kinds of sounds from this mound of pounds as he munches.

He's like an All-You-Can-Eat winner,
Or a greedy gorilla at a banana buffet for dinner.

Eating swell, sounding like a lion who caught a gazelle.

It's the bus bully Hank; probably sitting alone, because he smells.

With crumbs on his chin, Sloppy Joe sauce on his cheek;
If he gets any bigger, he probably won't see his feet.

There goes Mitch! My classroom itch—
With a couple of bully buddies and tater tots they pitched.
Green peas they plucked, and broccoli they chucked.
Some got hit in the face, in the neck, and in the gut.

The bus idiot is with him, Mr. Pimple Juice.
Mr. Fart sounds and eyelids flipped around abuse.
The window clown is with him too,
Asking around for some tissue
Because the snot from his nose is an issue.

Mr. Fried Chicken Freestyle is with him.
The hat on his cornrows had the dirties brim.

He had scratches and scars all over, from limb to limb.
What he wore was baggy, since he is extra slim.
He must weigh 10 paper clips, but that thought is a whim.

I guess that's the crew.
They saw the other bully from the bus, Hank in the midst of a chew.

He is bent over, and his butt-crack is exposed.
No one said a word, as if he already knows.
It seems he doesn't fit in some of his clothes.
With small paper balls— there he goes!
The fool with the snot nose chose
To shoot some butt-crack free throws.
Not just two or three, but four in a row.
He missed one, but made three, like he was a pro.

Went on the lunch line to see what they were serving.
Already uncomfortable with what I'm observing.

People cutting this long line that was curving.
The closer I got, the food smell was
disturbing.
Smells like Sloppy Joes, or meatloaf burning.
The fart fumes from the boiled broccoli
started swirling.
I rather that, because exposing my bread,
butter and cheese got me squirming.
Passed a trash can, so my Haitian sandwich
I'm transferring.

Finally, at the front of the line, and received
my food tray.
My homemade food is in the trash, so today I
will pay.
Too bad this Sloppy Joe looked far from
gourmet.
It's like they threw ketchup on meat from a
cow they decided to slay.

Cautiously walked toward a table to grab a
seat, so I could eat.
I had an uneasy bully meet and greet;
Said their names are Mitch, Tim, Sam, and
Pete.
Oh no, I hope Mitch ain't here to do a
classroom tripping repeat.

Both his and the Pimple Popper's attitudes
were most elite.
Aggression toward one another, is very
concrete.
They kept shoving each other, as if for me
they compete.
I felt my temperature rising, like someone
turned up the heat.
Nervously felt the sweat from my pores
excrete.
Racing, like a car chase in GTA is my
heartbeat.
Their eyes were full of lies and a glare of
deceit.
Wish there was a way to retreat.
Suddenly, trapped from front to back, it
wasn't even discrete.
The distraction is complete,
Unexpectedly, one of them flip my tray and it
flew 6 or 7 feet.
Then-my Sloppy Joe meat

Landed in some girl's hair, and the rest on my
clothes.
I was ready to explode,
And take the ill-advised road.
This is one of my all-time lows.

The sound of everyone's laughter slowed.
Only Myrtle offered to help, and the boy
whose hair snows.
My Angel was there, playing with her hair; in
it she had a couple of bows.
She glanced over in her Beyoncé-like pose.
Then, looked away, as if she just stuck up
her nose.
Another reason why this day blows.
I wanted to swing and catch each one of
these dudes with my elbows.
Break their kneecaps, I suppose.
Or shove my foot so far up their butts,
they'll feel how my toenail grows.

Ran out of the cafeteria, in a bit of hysteria.
Treated inferior like some disease or
bacteria.

Outside the caf door now, to get my
composure.
I go from anger to sadness, it's almost like
I'm bi-polar.
Three accidents, I mean incidents, in one
day; it's not even October!
I'm a punk, ain't got no testicles. I need a
donor.

I'm to blame! Should have swung on these lames,
and changed the game.
Instead, I'm embarrassed and ashamed;
With tears sprinting down my cheeks like the express train.

Snot bubbling, hands trembling like those people in the back of the building that smoke crack.
Face bright red, but you can't tell because I'm black.
Another blatant attack; already took much flak.
The "Biggest Loser," it would say if they had made me a plaque.
*How do I stop that? Is there something I lack?*
*Am I that much of a dork? I don't think I'm that wack.*
*How do I avoid the third rail, while walking on the train track?*
*How do I stand under the basket, and not get dunked on by Shaq?*
*Is there a way to pass the wolves and not get killed by the pack?*
*It's like I'm a plate of ribs, and they're waiting to tear up the whole rack.*

# BATHROOM BULLIES

## Chapter 5

Went to the bathroom to get cleaned up.
I let out one more cry, but made sure the
door is shut.
*With so many eyewitnesses, where's the help
from an adult?*
*Is it 'cause I'm new? A dork, but so what?*
*Is it coincidence? Is this my fate, or bad luck?*
Hope no one is in the stall doing number two,
and feels that I will interrupt.
I tried to get a paper towel-what do you know,
machine's stuck!
Then, put my hand under the faucet in the
shape of a cup;
To wash the stains out of my clothes, but for
sure this day sucks!
Unzipped my pants to get a better angle and
my shirt is untucked.
The hot water came out slow, as if thick like
syrup.

The cold water is harsh, the way the geysers erupts.
I can feel what's good inside me becoming corrupt.
I'm having visions of vengeance and violence, raw and uncut.


By the door I heard a whisper, so I pulled up my zipper
A little too fast, I think I clipped my thing—
I'm guessing, it's not a blister.
The sudden pain made my whole body quiver.
Afraid to look, might make the blood drip quicker.
It could be a scene from a horror movie or thriller.
Felt like part of me was a victim of Jeffrey Dahmer or Jack the Ripper.
Looked down and luckily I didn't cut much, just a sliver.
Stuffed my underwear with some tissue to contain the bleeding, then looked in the mirror
to see if it looked puffed up or noticeably bigger.
From behind the door thought I heard a snicker.

I shut off the faucet, I couldn't hear, not a good listener.

Walked toward the door and what did I see?
Mitch and Pete snooping and peaking at me.

Like Peeping Toms,
Hiding like Guerrilla Soldiers from Vietnam.
I felt the hairs stand up on my forearms,
And I tried to stay calm.
Hoping there wouldn't be much harm.
I'd rather one of those old school beatdowns from my mom.
Saw a bottle; this is a great time to pull the fire alarm.
In Mitch's palm, appeared to be a stink bomb.
They shoved me to the floor, fell in some substance like flan.
This is just like those stories from bullying.com.

He broke the bottle on the floor,
By my feet, then closed the door.
It took a couple of seconds before the stench began to soar.
It's more than barking— it's a roar!

Smelled like skunks and doodoo clumps galore!
The smell is all over me, not just on the
clothes that I wore.
I can't take no more!
Anger and sadness, seeping deep into my core.
Therefore,
*I'm going to find a way to prevent this*, I swore.
Protect what's left of my self-esteem, which
they tore.
If I was keeping score, I would have 0 to
their 4.
It's like I'm a Boy Scout, and they're in the
Marine Corps.

I can hear the leak from a pipe drip in a
bucket.
Tried to open the bathroom door, but I
couldn't budge it.
Gave it a shove, but didn't nudge it.
Guess I misjudged it.
*Where's my dork super strength?*
Wish I could summon it.
Ain't got no muscles, my flex is on a budget.
Plus, I know who shut it.
Mitch and his puppets;

Behind the door practical joking.
This is the reason why it won't open.

I'm not struggling no more. I quit! I'd rather sit.
But not on this pee-stained toilet seat, I'll stand for a bit.

And contemplate these heinous acts I want to commit.
I feel like pressing charges, but I'm sure they will acquit.
Wish I could drop out of school, but Mama would never permit.
Next, I changed back into my Dork Super Suit before I split.

All of a sudden, I heard the sound of the school bell.
Gave the door one huge shove— and then I fell.
Landed face first, like I slipped on some gel.
They weren't there; they ran away as if running from the Cartel.
I turned around, hallway packed like a roach motel.

Nothing but students and school personnel,
And Mr. Charles who started to yell,
"No pics, and put away your cell.
Keep it moving, and who we gotta expel?"
Then, the stench began to swell;
And everyone could tell,
It was me who was to blame for that awful
skunk smell.
Another disastrous moment from a day of
hell.

Everyone held their nose, and their breath, I
suppose.
Someone said, "It smells like animals
decomposed."
Someone else said, "Diarrhea blows
and someone's intestines are exposed."
And— "That's the smell when someone's
butthole explodes."
Someone also proposed,
"Keep the bathroom door closed,"
and, "you need to get hosed."
I smelled like I bathed in sewer water, or at
the very least, soaked my toes.
Or fell in fertilizer that helps the way a plant
grows.

Stood up, and the hallway became a living nightmare.

Nothing but stares. I'm fully aware, life isn't fair.

Felt like a square surrounded by circles and triangles from here to there.

Like I got some kind of disease that's considered rare.

Full of despair, like a bald polar bear who can't grow hair.

Or sitting on the bench with an ACL tear.

Like an alien, who landed in the middle of nowhere.

Or stranded on a deserted island without a boat or flare.

Maybe stuck in solitaire without a prayer or air.


I picked up the pace; I wanted to leave this place.

From behind the stairs, principal Hurst popped up in my face.

I thought to run for a second, *could I escape his chase?*

But he was too close for comfort— he violated my space.

Took me to his office with a look of disgrace.
Oh no, I think I'm gonna catch a case!
Can't even say it's because I'm black, since he
was of the same race.
The whole entire day, I wish I could erase.
If this was "first day dues," I think I had
more than a taste.
We both sat down, he spoke, his voice filled
with base.
He had the ashiest knuckles and his long
fingers are interlaced.
He also has different skin tones, as if he
were a cut and paste.

He has a beard like a Christmas tree skirt.
Underneath his suit, he wore a crisp white
shirt.
Big nose and cheekbones makes his thick
mustache perk.
Bushy eyebrows and one eye seemed lazy, like
it was overworked.
One is full of energy, the other seemed to
have none to exert.
One eye is healthy, it's hard to see, but the
other seemed hurt.
Because his glasses had some tint in them,
the fact he's hiding something is overt.

His hairline curved around like a dirt road in the desert,
And with those ears miles away, he can hear a concert.
He threw out facts in spurts, like he is an expert.
Said, "It's likely you were caught in the wrong place at the wrong time by some jerk."
It seemed pretty obvious to him, the pain inside me lurked.
"You're not a trouble-maker," was the opinion he'd assert.

Hurst cleared his throat, and spit when he spoke, so my face was drenched.
Asked me questions about the scent, while his eyes watered from the stench.

I didn't snitch, "I saw nothing" was my argument.
"Someone threw a stink bomb, but I didn't see where they went."
He said, "What will probably happen now, I can prevent."
Asked if I'm sure, I said, "One-hundred percent."

Then, he opened the window and checked the air vent.
Sprayed air-freshener, till the whole bottle was spent.
Then, called my mama to save himself from the torment.

After the first day from hell, I didn't want to go back to school the next day.
But being home with my mama alone, I knew exactly what she would say.

"You let those boys do that to you, and you did nothing to them back?
If the school ever call me again for something like that,
I'll beat the black off you with a hot wheel track!"

I knew she was only kidding, but with that belt she gave the nastiest whipping.
Even though at home there's rarely any hitting.
But when it goes down, like a ninja she be flipping.
Switch-picking, butt-whipping and kicking—
while I'm running and skipping, and dodging and dipping.

Then have difficulty sitting, and over there in the corner sniffling.

For the remainder of the week, to not be seen, is my whole technique.
Avoid the dude named Pete, with pimple juice on his cheek.
Avoid the snot nose dude; and Mitch, with his caveman physique.
Make sure I don't speak, even if they call me a geek.

Can't forget Hank, whose stench should have its own seat.
Around each corner I'll sneak, and don't get caught in the street.
If confronted, retreat!
Because it's a definite defeat,
When you're four feet and petite,
Some losses you just gotta eat.

Somehow I survived the rest of the week in the public school system.
Thought my strategy worked, but they had turned their attention to some other victims.

Heard someone locked Carl in a locker, or was it a closet?
They put fake bugs in Susie's lunch tray, and I heard she lost it.

They put ink in Myrtle's Pepsi can, and her teeth were black for days.
They put a sign on Stanley's back that says, "I weigh less than a bag of Frito Lays."

They spilled baby oil on the floor and made Fernando land on his back.
They even caused a flat on the wheelchair that belonged to Matt.

## Chapter 6

By the next week I had gym again, a class I
used to love.

But today we have the fitness test, which
some of us are scared of.

Like the nerdy, non-athletic kids, who fall
when you give them a shove.

The overweight kids; waist high, they can't
lift their legs above.

First person I see is my gym teacher, Mr.
Whiffersnuv.

He's standing in the middle of the gym with
some tight workout pants that fit like a glove.

He had the biggest, fake-ish, front top teeth
that were whiter than a dove.


Yelling at the kids as they walk in, "Let's go!"
With pauses and long sighs, sounding like a
broken cello.

He has the biggest adam's apple, that looks
like a pointy elbow.

74

Below that was the wrong place for a private part to grow.

As soon as I saw them, my reaction was, "Whoa!"

Because they swung like the real ones, and even hung low.

Heard someone say, "It's Mr. Wiffer Balls!" Guess the others also know.

Why did it take me so long to notice? I must be real slow.

It was also hard to ignore the stinky sock and mothball smell, so
I went to get changed in the locker room that had a pile of litter in every row.

Some kids in the locker room are looking nervous, some extra shy.
Afraid someone will make fun of their underwear, and make them cry.
Maybe say something about their ashy legs that are always dry.
Afraid to pick up their heads and look someone in the eye.
Some looked around hoping for an ally.
Kids are flying in with their volume sky high.
Celebrating like they have fireworks and it's the 4th of July.
Gym is a boy's favorite class, guess we all know why.
My locker was stuck; to get it open, I had to pry.
With caution it opened, and I peeked through the darkness like a spy.
Anticipating something crawling out of nowhere, or that something would fly.

It felt like the most dangerous place in school.

Boys jumping on each other's backs as if one's a mule.

Tapping each other on the shoulder seeing who they could fool.

It's like these boys were jacked up on some hydrogenated fuel.

Making fun of each other's bodies to them it must not be cruel.

They made fun of the kid with the back zits whose name is Raul.

Almost everyone is in their underwear, in this environment it's impossible to look cool.

From what I'm seeing, there should be a sign that says "No Pulling on Nipples" as a rule.


As soon as I got out the locker room, I saw Simone standing next to her friend with the big butt.

Yeah her friend Heaven, who looks like she carries a switch blade, and is always ready to cut.

Then I changed my dork walk, to my best version of a cool strut.

Simone even looked pretty in gym clothes, and I started drooling like a mutt.

Started daydreaming of us kissing in the classroom with the door shut.
Saw butterflies and heard birds chirping, but it ended so abrupt,
By Myrtle who's in my face smiling, she always seems to interrupt.
Saying either, "Hi Daniel, how you doing?" or "What's up?"

The fitness test began with half of the class doing pull-ups and jumping jacks.
The other half, looked like they're gonna collapse.
A few doing extra and they need to relax.
Whiffersnuv is observing to see what everyone lacks.

Tim can barely do one pull-up; he's so skinny, you can see his rib cage from his back.
He just hung like a wire hanger, hanging from the pull-up bar, like it's a coat rack.
When it was my turn, I saw Simone looking so I gave it two cracks.
I struggled to impress her, I did two pull-ups — max.
There goes Myrtle with a solo of enthusiastic claps.

Hank managed to bypass the pull-ups for two Hostess snack packs.

Next, we had to do push-ups and sit-ups, and we were paired off in twos.

I was paired up with Pete, the only kid in the grade who had tattoos.

Pete did his sit-ups first, and I held his feet, while being disgusted by the view.

He had acne on his face, and through the holes in his tight sweatpants; he had them on his butt too.

The sit-ups made him fart six times; this is the wrong exercise for him to choose

Because it smelled like animal throw-up, or a hippo who blew a fuse.

Then, we switched places and the odor made news.

Someone said, "What's that smell?" and Pete's response was, "Daniel say excuse!"

Everyone looked, including Simone, and once again I'm accused.

Heard someone say "Diarrhea Daniel," but I don't know who, I don't have any clues.

When it was our turn to do push-ups, Pete and Tim switched partners, which had me confused.

While I struggled through my push-ups, Tim took off his dingy high top shoes.
Placed his feet underneath my nose with socks that were way overused.
I started to gag when I noticed puss from his toe oozed.
I almost passed out, it smelled like a funk tug-of-war with baboons and kangaroos.
He tried to get them to touch my lips, but I refused.
While he and Pete laughed, on my behalf they were amused.
Tried to get Whiffersnuv to see that I was being abused.

Then all of the sudden, Whiffersnuv went nuts.
Because Hank didn't even bother; he just lay there, flat on his C-cups.

Now we are onto the rope climb, the hardest part of today.
Mitch and Pete climbed six feet with no delay.
Took control of the rope as if it was child's play.

Or as if they're orangutan stunt doubles,
climbing for some bananas on a tray.
The rest of the class is seeing Pete's butt
pimples through the holes of his sweatpants
that are grey.
The athletic girls climbed two to three feet
while the rope swayed.
My fellow geeks and nerds, before they
climbed, they all prayed.

Probably wishing this was a math test, and
rather be writing an essay.
They put down their glasses and asthma
pumps, and got on their way
While you heard, "Let's go pipsqueaks!"
From Whiffersnuv say.
Did I hear him right, did he mumble that
someone is gay?
That would be bullying, too, if we took a
survey.
Not sure what's going on, but acts of kindness
he would betray.
He opened his mouth so wide to scold us, in
the back of his mouth you can see his tooth
decay.
He kept screaming; maybe he's mad because
he drives a beat up Chevrolet.

When it was my turn, attention I couldn't pay.
Before I climbed the rope, kept looking
around to keep my eyes on bae.
There she goes, in that same old pose, but
her glow is never passé.
I couldn't do much, the rope kept spinning
with me on it, like I'm in a ballet.
So scared, those nervous fumes I began to
spray.
When it's Hanks turn to climb, this time he
would obey.
Took a deep breath as if staring at death,
then said 'ok.'

First, he looked at the rope; probably
wondering, if it could hold the amount that he
weighed.
Turned his fanny pack around, and grabbed
on, much to his dismay.
Falling out of his fanny pack were snacks, and
a junk food buffet.
Some of us looked away, because Hank was
serving us some butt crack soufflé.

He tried to climb up, an inch or two at best,
Then, he slid off, and gotta rope burn in
between his boy breast.

It was time to run laps in a final timed test.

Some girls ran as if it's Baywatch, or a beauty contest.

Ran as if they're in high heels, or in a prom dress.

Those wannabe jocks, with their high sports socks were completely obsessed.

Grunting and growling at others as if they're possessed.

My fellow dweebians were looking like they're highly stressed.

Some passed out, some just quit, they were completely a mess.

Sam should run with some tissue, I would suggest

Because dripping snot in our path made running a dangerous quest.

A few slipped and crashed into each other, as if part of a slide fest.

I gave it my all, out of breath and dying to rest.

Simone gave a quick glance, but she seemed unimpressed.

I would have quit, too, if she wasn't here, I confess.

From behind, here comes Mitch— leader of the pests.

Shoved me to the floor, and I skidded on my
bird chest.
I was thinking, *call the police!* The dude with
the pin head and Popeye chin they need to
arrest.
He must have took a class and practiced
being a complete A@$ is my guess.
Then, I heard, "Stop, you jerk!" on my
behalf; another Myrtle protest.

Now, back in the locker room to change
before my next class.
It smelled even worse now; like feet, and
dirty underwear, perhaps.
It was so loud, it hit me like a speaker's
boom blast.
I tried to change as fast as I could, since
there are jerks in the forecast.

Before I can finish and jet past
Whiffersnuv,
Mitch ran up on me to apologize for the
shove.
Pat me on my back, trying to show me some
love,
Hands felt like he was wearing a glove.

After I listen to this pin-head, wide-eyed,
Popeye chin speaker
I put my foot in, and it was wet inside my
sneaker.

It was a distraction— he was acting— while
one of his boys did this:
As I walked through the hallway, all you
heard was squish.
Some are laughing, and snickering. What did I
miss?
Then realized "Diarrhea Daniel" is tape to my
back— what a diss!

# GOLDEN OPPORTUNITY

## Chapter 7

The rest of week two was almost through, it
didn't seem like I needed saving.
Despite all the stress,
Today there's a special guest—
Lizard Man from the zoo came in.

Lizard man was pretty cool, and pretty weird—
all in one.
He had a Joseph Stalin mustache, and with his
hair he wore a messy man bun.

His teeth looked like a closet filled with dirty
baby shoes.
His beard looks like the homeless man's that's
sleeping in the park next to the mushrooms.

He was very hyper, that might explain the
sweat stains underneath his armpits.
He had the biggest hands, and the dirtiest
nails; they looked to me like gorilla mitts.

His last name was German, and his first name was Sherman, but he told us all to call him Schmitz.

He had a Scottish accent, you know, the ones that wear a kilt.

He had a large head and scrawny legs— like a cricket is how he's built.


He had all kinds of snakes with him, and he handled them without a care.

He had boas, pythons, black rat snakes, and two other green snakes that were a pair.

He had all kinds of snakes and a few others that are considered rare.

He told us facts on top of facts, and a few dangers that we're unaware.

He had the python wrapped around his arm— we could pet it— but I wouldn't dare!

Some couldn't reach it, and some couldn't see, so a few stood up on a chair.

Lizard man did the best he could to make the experience somewhat fair.

Then, he grabbed the boa, placed it on his shoulders and everyone couldn't help but stare.

A few girls would scream, as if waking from a sudden nightmare.

And every so often, when the snakes got close, someone would slip up and swear.

Simone was scared, too, and she didn't bother to get any closer.
I wish she wasn't here, I'm terrified; but doing all I can to keep my composure.
Her friend Heaven's big butt was in the way, made it difficult for us to move over.
She was also completely nuts, she teased the snakes when Lizard Man approached her.
Even the boy whose hair snows for once was moving slower.
I guess the snakes seem more real than the snakes he saw on the poster.
Hank just stayed in the corner and ate snacks till it was all over.
I'm glad for that because he might have rattled the snakes with his odor.
The snakes were drawn to Pete— a face full of acne makes him look older.
The more I think about it, I can see why snakes would get along with an ogre.
There goes Sam whose head sits on his neck like a boulder.
He kept walking around, but didn't make a sound, and his head he should have kept lower.

Because I could have sworn, I just saw his
nose drip on the skin of a snake that looks
like a cobra.
Suzie kept asking questions; her mouth kept
moving like a motor.
And for some reason she kept her eye on
Simone, as if she needed closure.
Myrtle refused to touch any snakes; when
Lizard Man asked, she just said, "No sir."
And the one who put this whole thing
together, was my math teacher, Mr. Dozer
Who seems to be everyone's favorite teacher,
a real joker.
Always smelling like an ashtray, guess he's a
smoker,
With a hair piece that looks like a squirrel
that was dead since last October,
Who for once, is finally excited and looking
somewhat sober.

Mitch is one of those people I thought
nothing could ever scare.
You know he's always pranking and joking so I
kept my eyes open to see if he's there.
Ever since the first day, I watch my back and
do anything to prepare.

Then, I looked back, there he goes— with his eyes closed, like he was saying a prayer.
He was having convulsions like he was about to blow, and Mitch chunks would be everywhere.
Saw a puddle on the floor, by the sneakers he wore; OMG, he must have peed in his underwear!

Looked around the room and everyone was crowded in chaotic rows.
I thought Mitch was lucky, because so far it seems that no one knows.
Even if no one saw, I'm surprised the smell of pee didn't hit their nose.
Although it was loud, at times the pitch would have its highs and lows.
I'm also surprised they didn't hear the pee trickle down by his toes.
Even the people standing closest to him— should have heard it as it flows.
Looked back at Mitch again— he's still stuck in that same pose.
So, I guess he must have froze.
Thought for a second, of all the cons and pros.
This is a chance for payback to one of my foes,

And to feed this anger inside me that still grows.
Or perhaps a chance to make amends, become friends, and be one of the bros.
Butterflies in my stomach, I'm anxious and I'm sure on my face it shows!
I gotta do something, but with both choices, I'm equally opposed.
Times up! I gotta make a move, so then I chose
To go inside my briefcase, grab my apple juice and pour it on Mitch's clothes.
I said, "I'm sorry Mitch, I'll clean it up!" and saved Mitch from being exposed.

# psychology of a bully

## chapter 8

Mitch's interaction with everyone became
strange.
He said very little.
It's almost like he was invisible,
but I know he couldn't have changed.

He kept his head down, even when something
funny in class went down.
He didn't make a sound.
No more embarrassing pranks, or cafeteria
flanks; he's no longer being a clown.
He would avoid and get annoyed when his bully
buddies came around.
The most he'll do is give them dap or a pound.
And although they are big time jerks, Mitch
still wears the crown.
It seemed like shame he found,
And in fear and worry he was drowned.
He kept walking around with his face
scrunched up in a frown.

I guess that's what it looks like when an ego hits the ground.

He looked ready to escape and run straight out of town.

I don't really care, he's a big boy; I'm sure eventually he will rebound.


Back in class now and Witch Vanswoon is speaking.

Looking like she fell out the sky and landed her broom that's not for sweeping.

Her voice still torments me, feels like my ears are bleeding.

I can't understand how this kid behind me is still sleeping.

He makes it worse, cuz every so often, she's in his ear screaming.

Then she texted a pic of him sleeping to his mother, which had him steaming.

She called another kid's pops in front of the whole class, and he began weeping.

Stomach is growling, because it knows lunch is next, and I'll be eating.

They need to shut the AC off cuz I'm freezing.

I'm tired of writing down notes, what's this gotta do with what we're reading?

It doesn't matter what these kids write down, they'll still be cheating.

Trying not to make it obvious, at bae I'm peeping.

Every quick peek I take, my heart starts speeding.

Kept licking my lips, not to be sexy, they were chapped and peeling.

A couple of pervs siting behind Heaven gesturing squeezing.

Grabbed the pass and went to the bathroom, I feel like peeing.

I need a break, because I can't take all this boring teaching.

Pushed open the bathroom door and it's still squeaking.

Someone came from behind sounding like a grizzly bear breathing.

It was Mitch who came in, and blocks me from leaving....

I'm thinking, *uh oh, is this a beating?*

He asked why I didn't say anything, what's the meaning?

"After all we've done to you, double and triple teaming,

All the attacks, foolish acts, pranks and all the teasing.

You could've easily snitched but you didn't;
and it's intriguing.
You could have blown up my spot, instead my
secret you're keeping.

You spared me and I owe you.
What I'm trying to say is thank you!"


"I'll stop being a jerk to you, but I can never
be polite.
Did your mom put starch in your briefs? You
seem a little uptight.
"Diarrhea Daniel" I won't repeat or recite.
You probably don't believe me, and that's your
right.
Everything about me you probably dislike.
Man, we almost posted a picture of you on a
website!
I'll pick you on my team during recess, alright.
And even though I might be short in height,
Or the same size as a can of Sprite,
Let me teach you how to fight.
So if they mess with you, it's not a moment of
fright."


We both laughed at how he made fun of his
features.

Then he said, "Meet me after school behind the bleachers.

Come alone, and let's make sure that no one sees us.

And please take off those loafers, make sure you got on sneakers!"

"You mean, by ourselves, no students or teachers?"

How can I get out of this, maybe faking some seizures?

Maybe I should go, but hide in the distance, at least 100 meters.

I wish there was something I could drink for some courage, need about two liters.

This could be betrayal, like how the Senate did to Caesar.

Or is he sincere, because I'm not a believer.


I thought about it, and was getting so scared, my eyes started to tear up.

Every part of me felt this could be a setup.

What if they beat me down and no one's around for it to let up,

To the point where my face even swells up?

What if I start bleeding? Because it damn sure won't be no ketchup!

What if they kick me in the testes; as a man,
how can I develop?
I could use a disguise, some way to dress up.
I can't shake these dudes, they're like a rash
that always flares up.
Wish I had a friend, a sidekick or someone
with whom to pair up.
I decided to meet him, man up and pick my
head up.

Met him behind the bleachers, he was alone in
that location.
I wasn't being deceived or set up, to my
estimation.
Had on my sneakers, even my sweatpants in
preparation.
He started giving me some street fighting
(slash) boxing education.
He was doing a lot of talking, just
instructions, a weird one-way conversation.
He is going out of his way— guess he feels it's
his obligation.
He showed me a left hook, jab combination.
He showed me an uppercut, but my scrawny
shoulder couldn't handle the rotation.

He threw a punch, but before I could duck, there's hesitation.

I was terrified of being hit, that I froze from the anticipation.

I tried to do what he did, even the faces he made, but it was a poor imitation.

I tried to think of "Floyd Money Mayweather," cuz I can use some inspiration.

Pictured myself in a real fight, using every ounce of my imagination.

My pops wasn't a fighter, and it didn't skip a generation.

My pops is known for running, but I didn't want that to be my reputation.

Wondering why Mitch's eyes were so spread apart, affected my concentration.

Did I just punch myself in the face? Oh my God, the humiliation!

At one point, I almost hugged him out of desperation.

Did I really want to learn, or was having a friend my only motivation?

I wondered if he is really invested in taking part in this loser transformation.

After a while, I think he sensed my frustrations.

Figured we practice some more tomorrow,
maybe some different variations.
We ended up walking home together, because
we missed the bus, is my speculation.
And he shared things with me, that were far
from my expectations.

He told me about his mother, that he never
met— her name is Anne.
He said, "She had many bad habits, she's a
drug addict who use to smoke in the back of
a van.
A junky, and a drunk and I know having a
baby wasn't part of her plan.
She didn't want to be a mother and felt that
no one loved her, so she ran.
But not before she tried to sell me to this
man
I hear, for a measly five grand.
When that didn't work, she wrapped me in a
shirt and left me in a trash can."
"My father found me and raised me,
We had it rough for a 10-year span.
He has a temper, can't control his anger,
and handles problems with the palm of his
hand.

Some things he threw, other things he would slam.
Why my mom left, he could never understand.
He calls me all kinds of names, and says that she's the reason I am who I am.
He gets drunk every Friday night, and passes out, and the floor is where he seems to land.
Once I caught him in the bathroom snorting a couple grams.
Poker night with his friends is how he hangs.
While listening to Beres Hammond, is how he jams.
He never asks for anything, just demands.

"I hate that I don't know who my brothers and sisters are. I hate that I don't know who my mother is.
Aunts and uncles treat me like I stole their money. My father makes me feel like I'm not one of his kids.
I get so upset sometimes, feel like hurting myself at worst, or someone else at best.
Tightness when I breathe, like a John Cena kick to the chest.

I get so sad, feel like I'm about to choke,
Or like someone's big toe is lodged in my throat.

Or like I'm a punch line in a rhyme or a stupid knock-knock joke."

I said, "I'm sorry you don't know who your brothers and sisters are. I have a sister, you can take mine.
Maybe it's a good thing you don't know them, consider it a sign.
Me and my sister are always arguing, and we fight all the time.
I wish I had a brother, but it wasn't part of God's design.
I hate it when my mother introduces me with the, 'This is my ugly son' line.
Company would look at her as if she was blind.
Maybe she was trying to hurt me, instead of using a switch of oak or pine.
Felt like I wasn't even her own kind.
*She despises me*— are the thoughts that go through my mind.
I still hate her for it, it's whatever; I'm fine.
Thought of running away one day, but don't want to leave Pops behind.
Once, my sister did run away, for only a couple of hours, she was easy to find.
With no money, she was at McDonald's stuck in a bind."

101

I asked him, "Is that why you try to control your crew, and tell them what to do, you're afraid they might leave?"
He said, "You mean like my mother did? Maybe, kid, that's what I believe.

That's why I have my boys, they're the closest thing to family.
I humiliate others, I guess when I'm stressed and unhappy.
And it's the best way to keep others from hurting me.
It makes me feel strong, and feel better about what I can be."

I'm thinking, he insults everyone the way his father insults him.
He says, "I'm quick to get upset, like my father I bet. He'll throw me in the deep end of the pool, even though I can't swim."

I asked, "Does he help you with homework, sports or anything?"
He said, "Nah, he's too busy yelling and drinking."

Hmm, he beats up on people. In a way, that's all he knew. 102

He added, "I'm sorry if I ever put my hands on you.
Guess I'm a bully, because my dad is one, too."

Then he says, "Oh! By the way, you know why I'm so scared of snakes?
And why when I see them, I pee out a whole lake?
One time, I showed my dad grades that were fake.
As punishment, he locked me in my room while I was still awake
With a boa constrictor, and I couldn't escape,
Or find an exit to make.
Because, he also turned off the lights, which made it too terrifying to take.
And ever since then, the sight of a snake makes me sweat and my stomach ache.
Hands trembling like I'm in the middle of an earthquake.
Whatever courage I had, starts to crumble and flake.
Yeah it's pretty obvious, my fear is opaque.
Sometimes I dream my dad has died— then I awake.
I try to remember his mom is to blame, she used to call him a mistake."

# The Betrayal

## Chapter 9

From the first day of school, I became accustomed to losing.
Even did the best I could to convince Mama of moving.
It looks like Mitch and I are becoming friends; the school year is improving.
To our surprise, we have a lot in common with things we enjoy doing.

We like most of the same video games, like Mortal Kombat, Teken, and Street Fighter.
Our favorites are GTA, Call Of Duty and Darksiders.
We like shooters, action adventures, and even the games you role play.
We're not a fan of FIFA, but we can play Madden all day and NBA2K.

We both love Lebron James, but his hairline is an interesting case.
One minute he has one, the next time you see him, it's like it was erased.

We'll never root for the Warriors even though we're amazed by Steph Curry.
KD is a traitor, he left his boy Westbrook in a hurry.

Cam Newton is the realist, we hate Tom Brady and the Patriots.
Odell Beckham is the illest, and he use to play for the Giants, our favorite.
Even in wrestling, we think The Rock is the greatest wrestler that ever lived.
He says John Cena is a wiener and he almost once met the Heartbreak Kid.

Mitch said he is Jamaican.
Before my response, there was much hesitation.
Because in the past when I said I am Haitian, it came with much humiliation.
Some ridicule and all kinds of violations.
Some prejudice and some isolation.
We bring sickness and disease, is the justification.
It seems that Haitians are the black sheep or the hated stepchild of the Caribbean.
Besides Mexicans, the other poster child for illegal aliens.

Or, the last place you would want to go on vacation.

The only things you hear about Haiti if you're having a conversation

are, "Don't hurricanes and earthquakes always hit in that location?"

Or, "Don't hunger, I mean, starvation affect most of the population?"

Or, "Isn't Haiti the poorest black nation?"

And, "You guys place your hopes on banana boats for your migration."

And, "You use vibrant mismatched colors for decorations."

All we say is, "Sac pa se"— "what's up" is the translation.

Oh, can't forget my favorite: "Isn't voodoo the main occupation?"

So my story use to be: my parents are Haitian, but I'm Canadian.

I was born on a plane flying over Canada was my explanation.

People always made a face as if my story didn't add up to their calculations.

He said, "I thought you were American, or half loser and half retardation."

Got rid of my accent by the 3rd grade; I was terrified of the associations.

But my sister never denied where she came
from, so I use to act like there's no relation.
And I always hated it when I had to show my
Resident Alien identification.

He said, "We eat rice and beans everyday." I
said, "Me too, how do you do it?
Mama said it's the only way to keep from
looking like a toothpick."

He said, "My dad said you can't grow up to be
a man without that curry goat and jerk
chicken in your system.
On trips he puts it in my lunch bag, but I
throw it out because it's embarrassing."

I said, "Me too, and if Mama found out, she
would kill me!
She would say she wakes up at four in the
morning to cook and clean and make me feel
guilty.
Then she would come to the school, take it
out the garbage, no matter how filthy.
And probably shove it down my throat no
matter who's next to me."

The next day Mitch and I sat together in the cafe and it took guts.
I heard familiar voices getting closer and recognized the struts.
His bully buddies came over and Tim said, "Hey Mitch, did you forget about us?"
Pete said, "Why are you sitting with this dork? Is that your new dork crush?"
Hank said, "I see your little girlfriend every morning from the back of the bus."
Whole time I'm thinking, hope his mouth he shuts.
And ended up spilling my juice on my shirt like a klutz.

I sat there quietly, perfecting my one technique which is evading.
As each one passed me, to intimidate, my shoulders and back they're grazing.
If I did get up and run, would they be chasing?
Or is Mitch being here why they're behaving?
Pete flexed his bicep peak at me and started waving.
Sam walked back and forth, why is he pacing?
Tim stared at me and had his fist balled up like he was aiming.

Looks like he's the main one that needs restraining.

If this was my world, I'd take them all on in some gaming.

I'm the best at any video game, is what I'm proclaiming!

I watched Mitch and them go back and forth, insults they're trading.

They asked if we're best friend goals, are you upgrading?

Wondered if they saw Mitch helping me after school with some training.

Sam said, "Did you guys meet on that dating site, Online-Geek-Dating?

Mitch said, "Shut up, to get up and smack you is what I'm debating."

I'm not sure if they were serious, or just playing.

To me it sounded like his boys were hating.


Tim said, "Let's go, let's not break up this dweeb bro-mance.

But next time you go on a dork date, let us know in advance."


Later on that week, on the way home, we took our usual shortcut through the park.

You could hear the police sirens and the stray dogs bark.
McDonald's was on the right and to the left was an abandoned building that used to be Walmart.
And those dirty pigeons took a crap all over the McDonald's arc.

I saw girls double dutching, doing tricks like it was nothing.
It was Simone, Heaven and a girl who could have passed for Simone's cousin.
Some other girls talking loud while braiding and hair brushing.
When Heaven jumped rope, some guys watched, pointing while in full discussion.
It's some old creeps and some losers, but I ain't judging.
Many are b-balling, while arguing and cussing.
Taunting while dribbling, and while shooting they're shoving.
There's a bum on the park bench, his stench got a couple of kids fussing.

They told him to go take a shower, get a job, go do something.

Still asking if he can get some money, his stomach's grumbling.

The neighborhood junkie passes through itching and touching
Himself, while mumbling weird things— he be bugging!

There's a man over there, leaned on his car parked,
Looking like a black Tony Stark.
Seemed slick, but somewhat dark.
Like he had an iceberg for a heart.
Underneath his left eye was a scar, or a mark.
It seemed giving handshakes and making exchanges was his part.
Here comes a hustler selling stolen clothes and appliances in a shopping cart.
You gotta look away, so he won't come over, if you're smart.

Mitch says to me, "There goes Simone, go over there and say, hi!"
He caught me off guard with that, so I had to ask him, *why?*
He says, "Boy you're always drooling over her, a fact you can't deny.

If you like her that much, you should at least try."

"And what do I do after that? You can tell I'm really shy."

"Nothing, just keep it moving, as you walk by."

Is Mitch trying to set me up again, should I comply?

Not sure if this is an explanation I can buy.

He used to be one of them; on his intentions, you can't always rely.

 Maybe our friendship is the biggest set up, that would be real sly.

The closer I got to her, it became warmer than the heat in July.

All of a sudden, I started wheezing, sounding like a repetitive sigh.

Not looking her way, I'm looking down, even looked at the sky.

I was hoping for any distraction, even a cough from a random guy.

Even my walk got slower and slower, started creeping like a spy.

Uncontrollable nerves, and the urge to run away, I must defy.

My legs are wobbling, each knee and my left thigh.

I can barely breathe, like I will suffocate and die.

A new pair of testicles, I wish the Lord can supply.

What if I open my mouth and can't speak, and it's worse than a tongue tie?

Like there's a desert on my tongue and my throat is so dry.

What if I speak too low, even worse, what if my pitch is too high?

Ok, here we go, a few more steps, oh my!

When I finally said hello, guess what? She didn't even reply.

Matter of fact, she didn't even bother to look me in the eye.

I feel like bawling— so many people around— I can't cry.

Wish I had on a disguise— fake mustache, a mask, and some hair dye.

Mitch even snickered as it happened, I want to hit him, no lie.

Out of nowhere, here comes one his boys... buzzing around like a fly.


Tim walked up to her and asked if I was bothering.

But she just shrugged it off without acknowledging.

She could have spared me from the hate he appears to be bottling.

Then he turned and looked at me like raw meat and began slobbering.

Like he can hardly wait for that moment when I'm what he's devouring.

It seems as if something real violent he's pondering.

Perhaps which part of my face he prefers remodeling.

Like he was having visions of breaking my legs and my back they clobbering.

And there goes Pete— just standing there, posturing.

Staring and smiling, then it quickly changed to scouring.

And what made it worse, is that he said not one thing.

From the others, in insults I was showering.

Like my bow tie, I should consider retiring.

And that Dorks 'R Us is hiring.

At this point I felt like I'm half a pint, and over me they're towering.

How can I get out of this? Wish I had something for bartering.

114

Anticipating what's coming next, and knees are still wobbling.

Hope no one noticed these fears and tears I'm harboring.

And these butterflies in my stomach got me feeling like vomiting.

Whether to throw the first punch— or run— got my mind boggling.

Only move I got is to flinch from cowering.

I'm frozen; if I try to move, I'm either falling down or hobbling.

For a second to get some help, I thought of hollering.

Not knowing which side that Mitch would be honoring.

Then they said, "What up?" to Mitch, then looked at me and said, "Back to you again?"

Besides the usual, they had with them a couple of other hooligans.

Tim was all in my grill, and in the corner of his lip was that nasty white foam.

As he cursed, it dispersed, and on my face his spit had flown.

He had one side of his head in cornrows, the other side uncombed.
Behind him anxiously was Sam, Hank and another named Jerome,
Who still sat on his bike with his wheels all in chrome.
Things were getting intense, I sensed a dangerous tone.
There was blood in the water, so the others like sharks, they roamed.

Tim shoved me from the front, Sam shoved from the back.
Now the whole park is at attention and they spontaneously react.
 With buzzing and commotion, anticipating an attack.
At first I stumbled like a drunk, then got my balance back on track.
*What is about to happen, and where's my briefcase at?*
Pete stuck his foot out, against the ground my face went smack.
For about five seconds, my vision went black.
All I heard were voices and someone's knuckles crack.

My vision clears up, they've got me surrounded like a wolf pack.

Mitch jumped in their path and told them to leave me alone.
That's when I realized that I wasn't alone.
I guess getting jumped he won't condone.
And he started getting aggressive, because to fighting, he's prone.

He got in Sam's face close enough to see inside his mouth where there's plaque.
Said he ain't having that, and won't take any flack.
Fist balled up, nostrils flaring, and you can feel the tension stack.
The grownups are just looking, not getting involved, and that's fact.
As if they don't mind seeing a little fighting, is how they act.
At this point Hank lost interest and started digging for a snack.

Smelling like roast beef or salami cologne.
Then out of nowhere some kicks were thrown.
Then Mitch turned into a pain hurricane, spinning like a cyclone.

He caught Tim on the chin, and Sam on the top of his dome.
Then he slipped and dropped his cell on the paving stone.
He went to pick it up, then got punched in the back of his head shaped like a cone.

The punch was so hard, I'm sure everyone heard the impact.
I got off the ground and leapt toward Sam to try to make contact.
Tried to tackle him, did my best version of a quarterback sack.
I went head first—surprised my head stayed intact!

While in midair, I belted out a huge roar.
Like the final charge, during an outcome of a war.
He fell to the ground, I was on top, while someone else kicked me in the core.
I tried to turn around quickly to prevent those kicks to my back anymore.
Then Sam put me in a headlock move, (slash) DDT, (slash) figure-four.
Forced me to say, "I'm Diarrhea Daniel," or he'll choke me, he swore.

Mitch is still on the ground dazed, as if betrayal has fully grown.

Then out of nowhere, Pete forced his hands on my underwear, in my restricted zone
And gave me a super-stretch wedgie from my neck to my tailbone.

What's that Tim is taking out of his pocket, is it a phone?
No— it's hot sauce— they poured it in my crotch, through my pants it had shown!
Not to mention the burning sensation the hot sauce had on me was completely unknown.

Then, as Sam plummeted his fist into my stomach, I couldn't help but moan...
And let out a humongous fart that sounded like a bass trombone!
Laid on the ground making sounds like my appendix was blown.

Now my underwear is lodged in my rectum and heart stuck in my sternum is what I own.

I'm sick of these bully clones, with extra testosterone,
Looking grown, or like they're on some type of growth hormone.

I wish I could've seen this coming, this pain and shame I would've tried to postpone;

But instead we got jumped by these bully
punks in front of  Heaven and Simone.
I'm terrified and wondering, *how will I finally
make it home?*

# MAMA BULLY IS BACK

## Chapter 10

I heard someone say, "It's Mr. Diarrhea and the pisser."

Everyone laughed; then I heard it again— this time with more vigor.

Hearing that echo throughout the park was like a trigger.

It turned the look on Mitch's face, to that of a straight killer.

Like he was plotting revenge or had a foul message to deliver.

I am upset but it appears Mitch's temper is much bigger.

I'm more concerned with getting home before dinner.

So much pain, not sure if it's my kidneys or my liver.

They ran off, but for me they couldn't have left any quicker.

As Mitch and I just laid on the ground like litter,

His only response to them as they left was,
"Yeah, your Mama and your sister."
The hot sauce on the ground looked like a
bloody river, but thinner.
The neighborhood hustler helped, he said,
"Get up," in a whisper.
Then I looked around for Simone, wish I had
the nerve to diss her,
Wishing I had a dead rat to give her.
Because of her, I'm over here looking like a
real winner.
Can I get over this? I'm too young to be
bitter.

Now Mitch is confused and upset at what he
heard.
He played it off like it was completely absurd.
I assured him that I never said a word,
Not sure who else in the class might have
seen or observed
when lizard man came and what had occurred.
The back of the class smelled pissy, like a
street curb.
But you never know, my memory could've been
blurred.

Maybe no one saw anything, they could've just guessed or inferred.
Maybe we heard wrong, maybe their speech was slurred.
So he says, "*Now I'm the pisser.*" Not a name he exactly preferred.
Tell you the truth, I would rather be called *"pisser"* than "*watery turd.*"

I can feel the aftershock from getting dropped, and my fingers twitched.
I can still hear them call me "diarrhea," like on my back it was stitched.
I'm sick of getting dragged through the school year, like behind a truck I'm hitched.
Before this happens again, we should say something, is what I pitched.
Rat them out or have my school be switched.
Still digging out the wedgie, but it looked more like my crack itched.
Mitch said, "If I tell, my rep might as well be ditched.
*Nah, I rather revenge, it won't be me who snitched.*

Snitching does nothing except make things worse.

It makes your enemies commit more felonies,
I rather flip it in reverse.
Give them a taste of their own medicine,
watch what we disperse.
I'll teach you all I know, let's hit them where
it hurts.
What goes around, comes around; they'll get
reimbursed.
Snatch their self-esteem the way a crook
snatches a purse.
Put a dent in their confidence, and watch
their egos burst."
I said, "Couldn't we just talk to them, sit
down and converse?"
He said, "Yea, and when they punch you in the
face, send my regards to the nurse.
Because defending yourself is the only thing
that works."
I can see he wanted to fulfill this hunger for
revenge, or quench this so-called thirst.
I'm not really that comfortable with what
Mitch is saying, feel like I'm being coerced.
I asked, "Won't we get in trouble?" He said,
"No, because they started it first."
But I'm pissed off, too, and tired of feeling
like I'm cursed.

Tried to sneak in the house before Mama could catch a glance.
Looked both ways and listened before I advanced.
If she saw me, for sure she would question me about the red stains on my pants.

She might even hit me with the belt, make me do the itchy dance.
Didn't hear her voice or any movements, so I took my chance;
I tiptoed like a burglar, then did a pony-like prance.
Past the closet, past the window and the plants.
Accidentally kicked a roach motel that was also filled with ants.

I wasn't lucky, Mama stopped me in my tracks.
She was in the kitchen holding up two bats.
She must've thought I was a thief, here to steal our Haitian scraps.
She's standing next to the fridge and to the left is one of her Jesus stone plaques.
I should've known better; Mama can never relax.

Even when she's on the toilet, she'll clean the mildew in the tile cracks.

She said, "Where are you going looking like you were running laps...

Trying to avoid me, perhaps?

Why do you have red stains on your school slacks?"

So, I told her I sat on some ketchup and hot sauce packs.

She said, "Is that why your shirt is torn with missing buttons and snaps,

and you're smelling like buffalos, billy goats and a herd of yaks?

Boy tell me the truth! Nothing but facts—

No gaps, before I commence with the slaps."

See, Mama has several types of crazy.

Here's a heads up of all the ones you may see.

Right now she's on the first kind of crazy, her usual, once a day, Haitian mother rant.

She's reminding us how we're ungrateful and unworthy on cue like a chant.

How she wakes up at five in the morning to cook and clean,

By six, she's putting clothes in the washing machine,
And that she's been doing this even before she was a teen.
She said, "You got the nerve to come in this house and lie to my face like you're a grown human being!
I put food on the table, clothes on your back, am I really seeing what I'm seeing?
I come to this country to work for white people
for you," while pointing toward the window screen.
She's a slave at work and a slave at home— is how she paints the scene.
Here comes her second kind of crazy, now she's starting to scream
With one hand in the air, the other slapping her hip, like she's playing a tambourine.
Yelling out, "Oh, Jesus," to a porcelain Jesus-like figurine.
And jumping around like she's on a miniature trampoline.

After I told Mama the truth, she really started to flip..

So now we're on her third kind of crazy, and
it's a trip!
She's saying outlandish things and the
emotions quiver her lip.
Exclaiming, "They're gonna have to lock me up,
to jail I'm gonna have to be shipped!"
Going off about how they'll have to beat her
up, too, looks like she's losing her grip.
Says, they're going to have to kill her, but
instead of R.I.P. she ignorantly says "rip".
Now she's stomping her feet, banging on the
walls, making the paint chip.

We're up to her fourth kind of crazy, when
she starts rambling about how she saw this in
a dream.
Haitian moms always have a dream with the
weirdest interpretation of what they mean.
Said in the dream she's eating fried pork
(griot), a staple in Haitian cuisine.
Said they had ran out of hot sauce (piclese),
and it was also Halloween.
And that explains what happened at the park,
to her it seems.
I'm telling you, making ridiculous connections
between events and dreams— of that— she's
queen!

128

Mama became furious because Pops wouldn't wake up, so she decided to intervene.

She's on her fifth kind of crazy, throwing things like she's on the dodgeball team.

Threw a cup of water on Pops, who has that 'sleeping on the couch' gene.

Not sure if he was in a coma, or almost awake, or somewhere in between;

And she resumed with throwing slippers at Pops, as part of her routine.

Pops woke up upset in a way that I've never seen.

He was trembling, spitting on himself, and from his nostrils, it's as if he's blowing steam

While saying he can't take all of this throwing before he has another cup of caffeine.

Then the phone rings, and she says, "Ahlo, ahlo," so many times, at least 13;

Guess what? It's a bad connection, and it's her best friend, Sabine.


She exaggerates to Sabine about how I came home all bloody.

Clothes were all ripped and shoes were all muddy.

Didn't I just tell her it's hot sauce, why she acting all nutty?

It's her fault, for people wanting to kick my butt, making me dress like Chucky.

Whole family will know in a few hours; if it's just Sabine, then I'm lucky.

She's making things worse, it's bad enough I already feel cruddy,

And defenseless, like a kitten or little puppy.

Pops is by the couch putting his shoes on all fussy.

He's annoyed and pissed off, but in Mama's hands, he's like putty.

He tried to calm her down, and almost caught an elbow, trying to be all lovie-dovie.

Then out of the blue, saw my sister come out the bathroom, nose all stuffy.

Said she's been in the room and heard the yelling, but had to study.

She looks at me and says, "Why is your face puffy?

Who put their hands on you? That's my job, ain't that right, little buddy?"

Pops just pat me on my back, with his face unshaven and all fuzzy.

Mama was so loud, spoke on the phone like it was a must-see.

Then while on the phone, she started arguing with the neighbor, Mrs. Duffy,

Who was just as loud as Mama, oh by the way, she's also a little pudgy.

Yelling from her window, pointing and moving her head abruptly.

Apparently Mama was so loud, she woke her baby up in the cubby.

Mama didn't care and with her sixth kind of crazy, she got all huffy.

Waving a wooden spoon at Mrs. Duffy, cause she's a toughie.

With insults and threats, saying, "That's why your baby's ugly!"

If they argued any longer, Mama would be throwing hands, trust me.

Mama said, "We're going to the park to find these boys who committed these acts.

Going to snatch them and take them to their parents, dragging them on their backs.

Make an example of one, and make his lung collapse."

Told Mama not to go, I said, "Mama, please don't do that."

Mama is stubborn, she shut off the oven, and said, "Dadi we are leaving in 10 minutes, max."

Before we left the house, Mama decided to say a quick prayer.
Well... I thought it was going to be quick, but a Haitian mother's prayers has many layers.

She prayed so she doesn't get locked up for these kids she's about to hurt.
She prayed that I don't become a bum, a hoodlum, or a street-thug type jerk.
She prayed for safe travels at night when walking through the hood, because in the shadows, weirdos lurk.
She prayed that the bus driver wouldn't crash on her way home since he's never alert.
Now this is when the prayer makes a u-turn and starts to divert.
She prayed that my sister don't get knocked up by some little pervert.
She prayed that Pops ain't messing with a "Bouzin;" that means a woman who'll flirt.
She prays for Sabine's cheating husband's thing to fall off in the dirt'
With a couple of "hallelujahs" she would say in spurts.
*Does she think before speaking? Some things you just can't blurt.*

Now, she's praying she gets tickets to the
Sweet Micky Concert.
While praying for her supervisor, whom she
hates, to get sick and not make it to work.
My sister did her best not to laugh, but on her
face is a smirk.

My sister stayed behind, the rest of us got in
Pops' 1989 Toyota Camry.
My mother hates to drive, so when Pops is
driving, it's the only time he looks manly.
Pops was trying to stay calm, Mama started
complaining, said he is driving like a granny.
Inside Mama's purse, you can see the wooden
spoon she got from the pantry.
She had several weapons and belts, as if she's
militia, or infantry.

Mama kept bringing up old accusations, that
Pops is denying.
Pops started trembling again, yelling back at
Mama while he's driving.
Not sure if dad was crying, or if it was
allergies, since on one eye he's relying
Using pockets full of dirty handkerchiefs for
drying.

Now I'm getting scared, weighing our chances
of surviving
Because the car swerved a couple of times,
and it was frightening.
He almost hit an old man who jumped back so
fast, his fake teeth were flying.
Whoa! We just missed hitting another car,
utter disaster it seems we're defying.
What in the world is wrong with these two?
They must have heard heaven is hiring.
And he just ran a red light, like stunts in Fast
6 he was trying.
Now here come the sirens...though not
surprising.
*Pops, please remember you're a black man, put
both hands on the wheel or shots are firing.*
The shortest cop I've ever seen, up to the
driver's window he is climbing.
He asks for license and registration, but the
top of his head we were eyeing.
Pops did his best imitation of a respectful
citizen, even his accent he tried hiding.
Mama offered the cop some Haitian food in
tupperware, she's gotta know this is bribing.
But really though, she carries food in her
pocketbook, because fast food she ain't
buying.

He took the Haitian food, and let us go with a warning— swear I ain't lying!

When we got to the park, there was a car on bricks and another with four flats.
On the ground there was glass and broken syringes and we avoided them like thumbtacks.
The mosquitos and fireflies were having a territorial war with the gnats.
It was supposed to be cool and clear, but in contrast,
A warm sewer breeze is the only thing in the forecast.
Graffiti on the walls and on the concrete cracks underneath the train tracks.
At the park, Mama stood there with two belt straps.
Anything can re-trigger the crazy, I hope she dosen't relapse.
She is moving like a mother lion ready to attack.
With her thick Haitian accent, she asked around for the pack.
But the boys from school weren't there, just a couple of hustlers, hood rats and two stray cats

Rummaging through garbage and looking for scraps.

Two bums playing Cee-lo, or it could've been Craps.

Three boys in the corner busting some freestyle raps

And a couple of drunks talking and standing next to the bike racks.

They stopped and looked at Mama while wearing two dirty baseball caps.

Then Papa grew some ball sacs,

and told Mama, "Let's go, let the boy fight his own battles, let's see if he adapts."

# bully recruits

## Chapter 11

The very next day, I'm in front of Vanswoon's class...

Simone walks in, no acknowledgement, like I'm a peasant as she passed.

Heaven gave a look, and said "eww" with so much crass.

Her big butt blocked the doorway with all that mass.

You can hear Vanswoon speaking, voice sharp enough to break glass.

Pete walked in, looking for some girl to harass.

Hank was coming down the hall... inhaling some food— he'll probably have gas.

Mitch ran up, and he was a little out of breath; he must have been running too fast

As if he was running from a pit bull or from a gunshot blast.

"You still want payback?" is the question I asked.

Before he answered, one last breath he
gasped.
We also waited for Hank to walk inside—
since the area he takes up is so vast—
While licking crumbs off his fingertips, at
this time it's his only task.
Mitch said, "I know just how to get them
back, and we'll get to laugh last.

I have a plan, My G, but it must be immediate.
first we're going to give them names, make
them feel like idiots.
Make it catchy, My G, everyone should laugh
when they hear it
And contagious like a disease that's now
chronic.
Holding in their laughter like they're about to
vomit.
Make it memorable, My G, and make it iconic,
So it comes up in every rumor and every
gossip.
You'll know it's legit, if years later... they still
talk about it.
Make people forget their real names, My G,
like they're misfits."

Hold on, how many times is he going to say "My G?"

Within the last 30 seconds, I think I counted at least three.

What does "G" stand for, what is he trying to say about me?

Should I ask him?— He's got me wondering— hmm…. let me see.

Maybe "G" stands for "goat" or "giraffe"?

But that can't be correct according to my math.

Unless he thinks I smell like a billy goat and that I need to take a bath.

It could be that "G" stands for "gorilla", but if you ask me, walking around looking like an ape is more down his path.

Conceivable, "G" could stand for "genius", since my grades are pretty ok…

Or feasibly, "G" stands for "gamer", since I always beat him in NBA2k.

It could also stand for "garbage", because in real life I can't play.

"G" probably stands for "guy", that's what we are anyway.

He continued with, "Turn the names into a riddle, or rap, or rhyme
Or make it into a song with jokes combined.
The really sick kind, My G, a parody redefined.
Fully grimed, and a real bully design.
We'll probably get ticketed or fined
With nothing but violations, it would be considered a crime.
Make it a blow to the ego, put their self-esteem in decline
Line by line, send them a message or a sign."

Then someone bumps me, and normally it wouldn't bother me,
But I heard no "excuse me", and there is no apology.
Then another stepped on my toes, I guess no one can walk properly.
While another knocked my briefcase out my hands, they must not respect my property.

On the other side there are two girls holding hands— what's that about?
They're holding onto each other, like one another they can't do without.
Maybe they're going down the "keeping each other's hands warm" route,

Or is there a "boy with real hands" drought?
But I see a lot of girls do this, without a doubt.
"Dorks need love too!" I wish I could shout.


Mitch is still talking, not veering off of his cause
Stating, "We'll create a dance that pokes fun at their flaws,
Shake like we've got bugs in our draws, moving on all four paws.
Make it the most ridiculous dance they ever saw,
Jerk whatever works, My G, uncut and raw.
Break all kinds of dancing rules and motion laws,
Make even people with no arms want to applause.


Then draw pictures of them and exaggerate their features,
Make them look like a cross between humans and creatures.
Something you'll find under a rock or from underneath the bleachers,
Or an over-mutated mutant in some high top sneakers,

141

Or characters who had too many bad plastic surgery procedures."

Then I see this student walking around from the corner of my peepers...

Who always looks lost and confused, and sometimes even weirder.

Who's constantly being made fun of, at someone else's leisure

Don't know his name, but they called him "weiner"

And because of his front two teeth, they said he's a beaver.

Maybe because he's small and a lot weaker?

Perhaps because his clothes look a lot cheaper?

As soon as the jokes come, he changes his demeanor.

He hysterically laughs like he's having a seizure.

Confuses his attackers; is he being sarcastic, is he crazy? Nah, neither.

Did he outsmart them? It seems the jokes stopped, as he sprints off like a speedster.

Now back to Mitch, who had a look on his face, that had the intensity of a preacher.

He spoke in a loud whisper not allowing his pitch to get steeper.

He said, "We'll also use social media and the internet to make it spread,
Make them leave their emails and texts unread,
Afraid to check their Instagram and Snapchat to see what lies ahead,
Because embedded within will be embarrassing memes and threads.
Let's think ahead, My G, and make them dread
Every minute they're not sleeping in their comfy little beds."
I'm noticing there is some snickering, from Juan and a kid named Ted.
As they passed us, one said, "Diarrhea and the pisser, I'm dead!"
I assumed they heard what happened at the park, but I ignored it as I tread.
It could be just rumors, no facts, just alleged.
I think Mitch heard it, too— he's looking a little on edge.

He finished his pitch with, "We'll isolate them from everyone else in school,

Make them outcasts, My G, even in class
everyone will see who's a fool:
Tim, Sam, Hank, especially Pete who's a first
class tool,
Leak each one of their secrets, break an
unwritten rule.
Make them not trust one another; I know it
sounds real cruel—
The victims become the puppet masters, we'll
redefine what's cool."

"We can't do this alone, with just us two, we
must act fast.
Let's organize and put a team together of
everyone they bullied in the past."

"We'll get Quiet Carl, who we shoved in the
gym locker in only his boxers and shut it
closed."
I said, "You mean the kid with the head like a
brussel sprout and the gorilla nipple on his
nose?"
But it's not really a nipple, just one of his
moles.
Always dressed in church clothes,
Oxfords on his feet, everywhere he goes
Even in gym, and with every ball he throws.

I heard during a fourth grade spelling bee he froze.

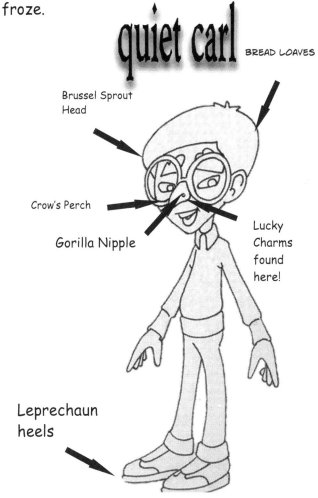

quiet carl

BREAD LOAVES

Brussel Sprout Head

Crow's Perch

Gorilla Nipple

Lucky Charms found here!

Leprechaun heels

Mitch said, "He looks like a leprechaun who wears heels on his soles.
Either that, or he's the only leprechaun that grows.

His pops got that beat up car, nothing but smoke it blows.

His nose is so big, it's made for perching by crows.

Lucky Charms might fall out of it, when it blows.

His hair looks like two pieces of bread loaves.

Always sits in the front of the class and in the first two rows.

Always says, 'I can't be late' and 'I'm sorry' When he did nothing wrong to his foes.

Always flinching and looking paranoid because of bullies, I suppose.

So much information on insects and mammals he knows.

On a class project he created the funniest names for the hominids he chose.


He wears those huge glasses, that look like bicycle wheels,

Or the steering wheel on an automobile.


Although he is quiet, he wants to be a standup comic.

So he can definitely help, I know it's ironic."

"Let's get Stick Figure Stanley. The kid we said weighed less than a bag of Frito Lays. That's not a six-pack, that's his rib cage; and when you blow on him, he sways.

Probably looks like the letter /x/ when he lays,

Basketball is the only sport he plays

And underneath his armpit is where his ball stays.

But it seems, not even the ball he outweighs.

He must be on a grass diet, like he graze.

He must think looking hungry is cool, hope it's just a phase.

Perhaps he eats only every other day, or just on Tuesdays and Thursdays.

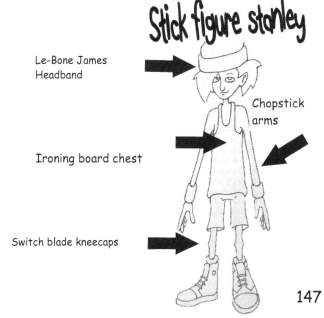

Stick figure stanley

Le-Bone James Headband

Chopstick arms

Ironing board chest

Switch blade kneecaps

147

He gotta have a tapeworm, heard he's allergic
to mayonnaise.

More than likely shows up invisible on x-rays.

And if it's his job to weigh single digits, he
should get a raise.

Or whoever's job it is to feed him should be
fired, and not get what it pays.

He seems laid back, but he's in the special ed
class, so there might be delays.

But he can draw anything you want, and in
different ways

And he always seems to have on a new pair of
J's.

'It's all good in the hood' is his catch phrase.

He has a headband on because he likes LeBron,
whom he portrays.

He has grasshopper legs, chopsticks for arms
and a sleepy gaze.


He looks like one of those skeletons that
hangs in the doctor's office
and under wind resistance, you'll find him in a
thesaurus."


"Myrtle Metal-Mouth would help us, too,
The one in Mrs. Vanswoon's class that you sit
next to,

Who sits on the opposite side of the girl who eats glue.

The one that's in love with you, you know who.

Always staring at you, admiring the view.

 Like you're made of cake, and she wants not just one piece, but two.

Don't act like you don't have a clue.

Why do you think she always sticks up for you?

 Dorks she must be into.

Always saying, "leave him alone you jerks" to me and the crew.

If you farted, she'll probably take blame and say, "It's me who just blew."

And she would probably thinks it smells like roses, instead of poo.

I think she's Indian or from Pakistan, your boo."

"Oh, you mean the one with the Marge Simpson hair-do?"

He said, "Braces are like barbed wire from a prison, cemetery, or zoo.

And when she smiles, it seems like a pile of on soda cans she can chew,

And she can probably deflect bullets when she smiles at you.

149

Heard she can write songs in several languages, who knew? She's on the debate team because she loves to argue.

And she'll kick the crap out of you with her steel-toe shoe."

I said, "What's up with the gloves? Is that new?"

"I don't know, she always has them on, not sure what she's been through.

And as far as if we put ink in her Pepsi can... it's true."

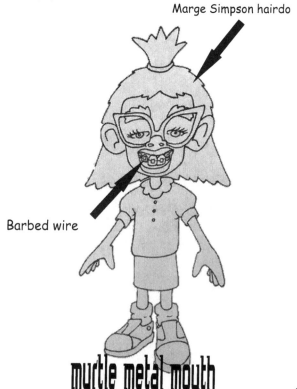

Marge Simpson hairdo

Barbed wire

myrtle metal mouth

He continued with, "let's get Social Media Suzie, who talks nonstop.

She'll spread your business from school to the block, from church to the pawn shop.

The one with the eyelashes that look like wings from a crow that strayed from the flock,

Who on top of her head, she has a bushy blonde mop,

like a Halloween wig or prop.

Her chin looks like a baby's buttock.

Around the throat area, she's part bullfrog, but she doesn't hop.

And the gums in her mouth are high on her teeth, pulled up like a sock.

She speaks with a lisp like half her tongue is severed or chopped.

Blonde Mop

Crow wings

Baby shoes

Baby buttock

*Suzie social Media*

She always says, "I don't feel too good," like
she's ready to vomit the food she got.
She'll say, "You won't believe what I just
heard!" Then a rumor she'll drop
And if her cheeks inflate anymore, they'll
pop.
Her stomach falls over her belt as well,
because her Kids 'R Us sweater just crops.
Because it's too small, the store probably
didn't have her size in stock.
She wears it anyway, not sure why there's
always a little throw-up stain on top,
But after putting those fake bugs in her
lunch tray, if she speaks to me... I would be
shocked.
He's always making threats, since her daddy's
a cop.

Let's also get that annoying kid in the wheel
chair, in the honors class...
Yeah, Matt.
Heard him telling stories about how he ran
over his neighbor's cat.
Then he laughed at how he heard it's neck
crack.
He has those frisbee ears that gets in the
way when he tries to wear a hat,

And his eyebrows look like two roaches stomped on his forehead and went— splat!

His teeth look like little pellets used in combat.

And he ain't shy about showing them, since he loves to chit-chat.

Heard he's a genius with the laptop; anyone and anything he can track.

Websites, webpages and even emails he can hack.

He might be the best one to get, he'll make the biggest impact.

Satellite dish    Dead roaches    Pistol pellets

MATT THE HACKER

Hope he doesn't know that on his wheelchair tires; I'm one of the ones that helped make it go flat."

I said, "Bullying a kid in a wheelchair? That's where we at?"

Mitch said, "But he deserved that,
Because he's a brat.
We had to get him back.
With his wheelchair our kneecaps and chins, he would attack.
And would also run over our toes, wherever he goes, then laugh and call Hank fat."

I said, "What about the kid with the weird dance technique?
He has flakes on his belt buckle, which is kind of unique.
Who pop-locks in the lunch room, on the bus and in the middle of the street?
Is that dandruff on his shoulders and down by his feet?

Looking like ash that fell from a volcano."
Mitch said, "Oh, I think his name is Fernando.
Always in a jumpsuit, in his B-boy flow.
We call him 'Flakes,' cause when he dances, his hair snows

154

And is always laying to the left like he was in a
tornado.
His hair is smeared on his forehead like he
used glue or mayo.
Hanging from his lips are two dominos.

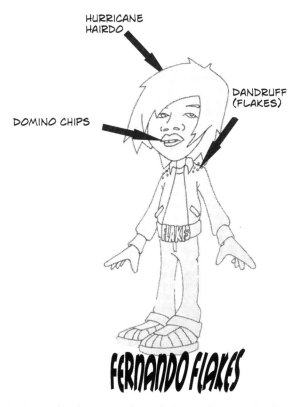

HURRICANE
HAIRDO

DANDRUFF
(FLAKES)

DOMINO CHIPS

FERNANDO FLAKES

I thought he was Dominican ,but nah, he's
from Puerto Rico.
He's in ESL, and always saying things are
'bueno.'

155

He says dancing is life, and thinks all his moves are 'fuego.'
Only guy friend he has is a kid named Mateo.
The rest are all girls, I wonder why that's so?
He's too nice to help us, it's almost like he wears a halo
And he always wants to dance battle. If he asks, just say no."

Mitch said, "But who should approach them? It can't be me, My G.
I use to be the main culprit. I'm the last person they want to see.
Daniel, you should do it, they can relate to you.
We've put you through a lot of the same things we put them through."

Then I said to Mitch, "Wouldn't it be more believable if you're the one who spoke to them?
Since you used to be our enemies' friends, I think that's something they would comprehend.

And what would I say, 'Hi...
Would you like to join Mitch and I...

In a plot of revenge, but I can't promise you won't die...'
Boy that sounds like a lie."

Mitch respond with: "Just approach them and ask if you can speak with them, but I will do all the talking.
Because if I'm the one who approaches them, they'll run away like I'm stalking.

We'll approach them right before lunch begins,
right outside the lunch room, My G, before they
walk in."
I said, "Ok, later then..."

# The Proposal

## Chapter 12

Mitch and I both flew out of class right when
the bell rang.
The annoying kid in the wheelchair was the
first one we saw, since he avoids crowds
because his wheelchair bangs.
The hallway was peppered with those kids who
love to hit the books, and never hang.
You know, the kids that barely use any type of
slang.

I called him over, "Hey, Matt!
You have a minute to chat?
We have a plan to share with you and it
involves some payback."
He said, "Sure, we can chit chat."
Then closed the laptop on his lap.
He looked at Mitch and said, "As long as I can
use my wheelchair to make this fool's
shinbone crack."
Then suddenly a smell hit my nose like a bat.

Not sure who it's coming from, it's kind of hard to track.

Smells like someone's intestines are feces-packed.

I feel like I'm completely surrounded by it from front to back...

This smell has my nostril hairs in the midst of fearsome combat.

This sewer funk from someone's butt who stunk has us completely trapped.

I know they smell it, too, but they didn't bother to react.

Maybe Matt has a colonoscopy bag underneath the cushion he sat.

Or perhaps  Mitch sharted and it's dripping down his pant slacks.

But, oh noooo, I'm 'Diarrhea Daniel'... I get automatically blamed if someone smells crap.

Whoever smelt it, dealt it, and I won't admit to that.


Matt had that look on his face like he had something unpleasant to share.

He has a little fight in him, not someone you can easily scare,

Although he is considered a square.

I wanted to ask him how he got in the wheelchair, since I'm unaware.

I heard he got in the wheel chair because of a disease of the spine and the nerves it impairs.

Mitch said he heard it was because of a car accident, his mom sued and now they're both millionaires.

If he can't walk, why are they so dirty, the sneakers he wears.

It's to the point where he's immune to other students' stares.

Then Mitch said, "I'm sorry for my part in what we did to your wheelchair.

"Yes, I was there, but I didn't realize how bad it would tear."

He is noticeably sincere and with his emotions he is shockingly bare.

"I know it's too late to repair, but I would if I could, I swear.

But it's not like a regular tire, you can't just put on a spare."

Mitch began outlining the plan, every single part...

He was efficient with his words from the very start.

*Ahh… you like that word "efficient"? I heard it*
*playing Madden; yeah, y'all thought I was smart!*
But anyway, Mitch needs to hurry, because in
a few we must dart.

Then Matt said, "Hold up for a minute, wait!"
You want me to help you? Am I hearing this
straight?
Daniel, this dude is using you, don't fall for the
bait.
He's not your real friend, to us he can't
relate."
So, then I told Matt what happened at the
park, since he hadn't heard the update.
"See Matt, even Mitch now, too, is dealing
with hate."
Matt responded with, "And I'm supposed to
forget what your boy and his goons did to me?
Nah too late.
You know how many nights I laid in my bed
crying, feeling deceived by fate?
My dad abandoned us, because he couldn't
handle my newfound state.
I wish I had my legs, instead of the money
people overrate.
Everyday I'm at school, it feels like a mistake.

I might sound sensitive, but these stares I
just can't take!
Some of you still had the nerve to ruin my
chair tires, for goodness' sake!
Even put a sign on my back with tape.
I'm jealous, you guys can walk, but I can't, so
I'll make your shinbones ache.
And what would I get out of this?" Matt is
still trying to debate.
Mitch said, "You get a chance for what you
create, to hold more weight."
Then something switch, and the proposal Matt
started to contemplate.

And it seemed like Matt might be starting to
care.
And what started as a mean mug has turned
into a strange glare.
Mitch continued with, "Join us and be part of
the plan, I assure you, we'll make things fair."
His eyes lit up like it was a game of truth or
dare...
Then a sadistic smirk cracked Matt's lips, as
if to say "Bullies, beware".
What's he got up his sleeves, maybe some
lives to tear?

"I'm in! Watch your shins!" Matt finally declared.

Once Matt agreed, next we were looking for Carl, and there he goes.
Rushing to class so he can sit in one of the front rows.
Wind whisking through his bread loaves,
While he's being led by his pickle-like nose.
Hallways starting to fill up now; some walking, some stuck in a pose.
Causing traffic to build up like a bended hose.
Yapping about what happened in class, or last night on some TV shows.
Boys talking about the girls they like, who came up and now glows.
Shoving each other into the girls, and then saying "Chill, bros!"
As soon as Carl saw Mitch, he anticipated kicks and blows,
So he shut his eyes closed.
Based on his experience with Mitch, that's what he knows.
Hence, Matt did most of the talking, so Carl's nerves he can finally compose,
And be able to understand the plan we are about to propose.

As Matt described the plan, a booger in Carl's nose is revealed.
As he inhaled and exhaled, it moved back and forth, like the wipers on a windshield.
Now I'm having trouble staying focused, since it came out of left field.

I wonder if he knows it's there, he's gotta feel it wiggle.
Moving around in that snout that's looking like a pale pickle.

Uh oh— he brings his hand to his nose— he must feel something!
Trying to act casual, as if it's nothing.
First he scratches the tip like it's tickling.
Then brush his hand back and forth, trying to avoid picking.
He must have knocked it looser, because now it's dangling like a string.
Then he turned his head like he was looking for something missing,
Just so he can disguise that inside his nose he's digging.
Eww— on his finger tip I see it cling!
Now he's shaking his hand, hoping on the floor it will fling.

164

What is he doing, did he wipe it on his pants,
am I tripping?
*Oh my God! Don't do it!* He did it, finger tips
he's licking.

I'm trying to refocus, as you can see, my ADD
is exposed.
I realized Matt made the plan sound
technical, like we were pros.
Then Mitch added, "And no more getting
shoved in lockers without your knitted church
clothes."
But Carl didn't think it was funny, and it didn't
settle his woes.

Upon hearing the plan, Carl looked very
confused.
Said he was lost and didn't understand how he
is going to be used.
Mitch said, "You want to be a standup comic,
right? We need names that will amuse."
Carl said, "You guys sure you want my help?
I'm usually the reason why people lose.
I wasn't that mad when they put me in the
locker, I just took a snooze.
I'm used to not having any friends, I accepted
it, so my life now is on cruise.

Even my dad would rather not have me and my mom around, if he could choose."
At first it looked like he was going to refuse.
Still flinching every time we made a gesture, like someone who's been abused.
And speaking of abuse, you can see that Carl's arms were bruised.
He's still saying sorry— for what? Who knows… Mitch said, "Whatever, you're excused."
Then we noticed increments of excitement from Carl began to ooze.
Mumbled to his self, "This is my chance," and became even more enthused.

Maybe he realized there was some payback he owes.
And I could also tell he wanted the companionship, so to help he chose.
Then Carl and Matt left, continued to lunch, since hallway traffic now grows.

Next, we saw Stanley, Mr. Arms looking like chopsticks.
On the way to his small class that had only 12 kids in it.
I wonder if they had 13, would that make the teacher quit?

166

Walking real slow, as if being late, his teacher would permit.
Wearing an overgrown jersey that didn't fit,
With a basketball underneath his armpit,
Two other boys walking behind him, trying to poke the ball out, but he had a super tight grip.
It must be something he's used to, he knows the script.
Once, they succeeded; they passed it back and forth, giving each other an assist.
One of them even dribbled it in the hallway, and tried to split.
Stanley anxiously said, "Don't dribble it; give it back, you idiot!"
Stanley eventually snatched his ball but almost slipped.
I said, "Come here, before you go inside and sit.
We have to talk for a bit."
There are two boys wrestling against the lockers; it was like watching a Doberman against a Pitt.
And because they were growling, I thought eventually one would get bit.
Here comes Mr. Charles, ready to resolve the conflict,

Yelling at the boys while firing heat-sinking missiles like spit.

Once the boys stopped, with random stories he's equipped.

Mitch, Stick Figure and I were close enough to hear it.

Talking about how he used to model and how he used to be ripped.

Mitch and I told Stick Figure the plan, the more heinous parts Mitch had to omit.

Stick Figure still wanted assurance that it's all legit.

Mitch responded with: "I doubt we get in trouble, but it's not something I can predict."

Stanley said he had a bad feeling about this from the 'get,

That he doesn't want to get setup like his brother, who's a convict.

He said, "There's a lot on my plate, since my brother left.

I was hoping the more I come to school, the better I felt.

But every time I turn around, on my back there's something I didn't expect.

And doing nothing about it and not speaking up, sometimes I regret."

He kept his distance from the door, acting like that wasn't his class.
Said he wasn't going in there, just walking past.
Maybe he's embarrassed, I shouldn't have asked.
I've heard the jokes, too, and the wise cracks.
I've seen how when they see you in a small class, you get harassed.

Stanley also wanted Mitch to admit
That it was them that put the sign on his back, then skipped.
He also appeared unwilling to commit.
And said, "All I can do is draw and play ball, and that's about it."

I asked him, "What's wrong? This is our opportunity, you're not the only one on your back who wore a sign."
At the end of gym class, 'Diarrhea Daniel' was mine."

Carl's sign said, "Don't worry, the tumor on my nose is benign."
On Matt's back, instead of "hit and run", they wrote "hit and crawl;" now that was a real crime.
They wrote "snowman" on Fernando's back, but they know it's not winter time.

On the back of Carl it said, "Be kind, and kick a leprechaun for good luck from behind."
Behind Suzie it said, "I don't gossip; I exercise my mouth, since I gave up on my waistline."


The examples I said to Stanley must have worked;
And I guess it reminded him just how much we got jerked.
And how we were always looking around the corners where bullies lurked.
At first he seemed upset, but then his spirit perked.
His posture straightened, his voice deepened, and with words he could assert:
"Ok, I'm in. Let's make some feelings hurt."

Then Mitch said, "There goes Myrtle Metal Mouth."
Always in a hurry and she scurries like a mouse,
With her pink glasses and a lime-green blouse.
Gave Mitch a nasty look, as if to her he's a louse.

But when I called her over, she started smiling.
She said, "I need to speak to you, too, Daniel—perfect timing!
There's a dance in three weeks, and it's you I'm inviting."
I was shocked… guess it's true that I'm the one she's admiring.
Oh no! There she is— walking like she's gliding.
Simone and her friend, Heaven; a princess and her bodyguard sighting.
Both hands on their phones, texting and swiping.
And the smell of their perfume is filling up the hallway and rising.
With a couple of pervs were following and spying,
Making gestures with their hands, who knows what they're describing.

Myrtle and Mitch gave me a look; my behavior they were eyeing.

Did they notice I'm sweating, or are their agendas blinding?

I'm embarrassed, and the thought of running into Simone is frightening.

Can't forget how she turned her back on us at the park, don't need reminding.

When Mitch began speaking, Myrtle ignored him, not surprising.

She even started texting rudely, but he kept on trying.

But I couldn't stop staring at her gloves while she was typing.

Mitch told her about our plans, and so far, she wasn't buying.

All kinds of details, she was inquiring.

"Who else is part of this," and "When is this supposed to happen?" She's prying.

"What is that gonna do? And "What if we get caught?"— at random conclusions she's arriving.

Hesitating she asks, "What do you need me for?" Mitch said, "Your writing.

We need songs or rhymes that are somewhat trifling.

I know you're sick of seeing people get picked
on and then hiding."
Myrtle said, "Everyday I see so many trying to
find ways for surviving.
I always try to say something to these idiots
and it's getting tiring.
I see how their victims feel afterwards, and
sometimes I feel like crying.
They don't scare me. I still do my thing.
I like how you guys are recruiting kids who
got bullied, and it's kind of inspiring,
Even though the plan sounds sketchy, I'm
leaning towards obliging.
Though I can't stand you, I wouldn't mind
having part in these bullies retiring."

Then Mitch said, "And Daniel will go to the
dance with you, if you help with this uprising."
And in that moment— I felt like dying!
I'm thinking, *Why is this dude using my life for
compromising?*
Myrtle is one of the weirdest girls in school,
and there's no denying.
She makes out with her pencils, swear I ain't
lying.
Then all of the sudden, she said, "It's a deal,"
and that, "this is exciting!"

Suzie was one of the last ones walking toward the cafeteria door.
She's always late, she stays back to wait,
To talk till your eardrums get sore.
Most of what she says, you just gotta ignore.
Hope she's getting fashion tips for the tight clothes she wore.
She should stop shopping at Kids 'R Us, she needs new clothes in her drawer.
And if it's not that, bigger sizes she should explore.
She went on and on, some other girl she bore.
She was talking about exercise, because she is a little fluffy around her core.
Getting her to shut up appears to be a gargantuan chore.


Oh and another thing, she's constantly saying "literally".
Maybe she doesn't know what "literally" means… definitively.
She would say things like: "I heard she stuffed her bra, literally."
Or, "She smeared on a whole stick of lip gloss, literally."
Even, "One of her extensions fell on the floor, literally."

174

Two girls in the hallway were singing loudly...
Susie was like, "They must think they're the only ones in the hallway, literally."
Another girl was walking while reading and stepped on the back of her foot, and she responded irritably...
"She just ripped the skin off my heel! Literally!"
She "literally" needs to shut the hell up! Seriously.
Two other girls stood in the middle of the hallway talking, like they're seeking publicity.
They could at least be of use and direct this hallway traffic like a crossing guard; it would help considerably.


Mitch said, "Can we get a couple of seconds when you stop flapping your jaw?"
She smelled like vomit was seeping through her pores.
She looked at Mitch and said, "What are you bothering me now for?
Shouldn't you be somewhere robbing a bodega, or a liquor store?
Or kicking over garbage cans and peeing on the floor?
Perhaps giving wedgies and playing GTA4?"

Mitch gave her a look, like a lion trying to contain its roar.

I said, "We have a plan to even up the score, and you won't get fake bugs in your lunch tray anymore."

"That's not all you and your cronies did to me.
One of you said I look like a walrus that crawled out of the sea.
Another one of you said I was a blimp-of-the-year nominee.
You guys make fun of my weight, said I was pregnant with three.
I wanted to pepper spray each one of you, so you couldn't see.
You guys have no idea how upset I get weekly."

Mitch said, "We need your help, you'll make all the gossip spread and all the rumors pop."
Suzie goes, "What if I say I cannot?"
Mitch said, "Then be prepared for them stay on top.
And by the way, I found some pills of yours in the garbage, I almost forgot.
It was weird finding them there, but I figured, it must have dropped."

176

All of a sudden, it seemed like things got hot.
She began stuttering, as if she was searching
for a story to concoct.
She said, "D-don't t-tell anyone you saw them,
d-don't b-blow up my s-spot."
Mitch goes, "Hmmm... I don't know, pretending
that I didn't see something I saw, seems like a
lot.
Plus we have a simple little plan, that you're
trying to knock."

Suzie defensively, "Not everyone can be slim,
but that's what I'm trying to be."
Maybe she does all that talking to avoid how
she's feeling routinely.

She continued, "And what's gonna happen if
your rink-a-dink plan goes flop?
We do everything you say, and these bullies
don't stop."
Mitch said, Ok, fine, I'll pretend, but you gotta
give this a shot."
She said, "Alright, if we get caught, no
worries;  my daddy's a cop."

The dancing kid never came to the lunch room,
so around the corner we kept glancing.

We'll know when we see him, there'll be a 'flurries of ash' landing.
He'll probably have headphones on, zoned-out while jamming.
Then someone finally told us they saw him behind the gym, dancing.

We walked up on him and caught him off guard, so he seemed a little rattled.
He probably saw Mitch, and thought that he might get tackled.
Still wearing his favorite jumpsuit, looking like a Puerto Rican green apple.

Does he realize it's dirty? On it are all kinds of stains!
Grease spots, condiments and
all kinds of different grass stains remain.

We approached him, and I said, "Before we begin, we don't want to battle.
We have a plan, this bully crew we must dismantle.
And the goal is for their egos and self-esteem to become fragile."

*Are his headphones on… is he still listening to a beat?*

This dude is constantly moving like he has to pee, and it's ready to leak.
I wonder, does he move around like that in the bathroom, too, and pee on the toilet seat?
What if it's number two, is that the only time he's still, so the break off could be neat?
Does he move like that in the shower, doesn't he pass out from the steam and heat?
I've even seen him sitting in the cafeteria rocking out while he eats.
He probably sleeps with his headphones on, while the rhythm shuffles his feet.

Mitch said, "We need your help, and then we'll skedaddle."
Flakes said, "Bueno."
"Your inner Chris Brown, we need you to channel."
Flakes said, "Bueno".
"And once we're done, they'll no longer be a hassle."

Again he said, "Bueno".
Flakes said, "Ju tink no one will tattle?"
Mitch said, "No way, bro."
You can just look at Flakes' face and know he's the type to unravel.

179

Flakes said, "Wa ju gana do fo me? I gonna ask, ju can't say no."

"When we vinish de plan, ju two will battle me and Mateo."

Mitch and I looked at each other, then Mitch said, "We figured so."

Fine, it's a deal, "Are you down, Fernando?"

He said "Jes, dis is gona be 'fuego!'

# THE PAYBACK

## PART 1

## Chapter 13

By the next week, the plan was in full display
and it is profound.
Each member of the team came up to Mitch
and I, one at a time, on the school compound.
Showing exuberance, as if we're victory
bound.
Carl snuck up behind us in the hallway— at
first he didn't make a sound.
Spoke in a low tone, as if a secret he found.

Fiddling with his hands and constantly looking
over his shoulders.
*Does he plan on sharing what he did?* The
anticipation weighed like boulders.

Although he's shy, ready to burst inside him
is a class clown.
He started explaining that he remembers
things, by renaming nouns.

Most of it was on the fly, he didn't write them down.

Mitch responded with, "Like what?" He needed Carl to expound.

Carl said he renamed streets and key places in the town.

Said he calls our school "The Clinic" because it makes him sick, since there's always bullies around.


I asked, "What did you call the barbershop?"

He said "Guess...

There are two new barbers there and they're a hot mess."


"Ahh, did you call it the 'Chop Shop?'"

He said, "Nah, not that...

I call it the 'Recliner' because they push your hairline back."

I asked, "What about the train station or the bus stop?"

He said, "The train station is 'America's Got Talent' and the performances be hot.

The bus stop is the 'Weirdo Drop'.

One dude had a whole argument with himself about what he ain't got.

And everyone else be looking like, 'are one of these cars going to stop for me or not?'"    182

He said when company comes over, he called his dog the "Crotch Sniffer".
When he's with his other dog friends, he renamed him the "Butt licker".

His mother always wears a wig, so he calls her "Oprah Wig-Free".
If I did something like that, Mama would kill me.
Probably light me on fire and rename me "Extra Crispy".
OMG! He even called his cousin who's half black and half white "Fifty"!
Then he went off on a tangent, started telling us jokes about poop.
Guess he must have been practicing a "stand-up" comic routine, as if he's in front of a group.
Mitch and I just looked at each other, because he threw us for a loop.

He said, "There's Invisible poop, that when you wipe, the toilet paper is clean.
The 'Pop A Vein' or 'Neck Strain' poop makes you wanna scream.
The 'Sequel' poop— right when you think you're done-it comes back like Mike Myers from *Halloween.*

183

Next the 'Ninja' poop; you feel it come out,
look down— and there's nothing in between.
The 'Muscle Bound' poop— so big they look
like the biggest baby parts you've ever seen.

Obviously the 'Cliffhanger' poop— just hangs
there and won't drop
While the 'Bougie' poop, you think would
smell, but does not.
Of course the 'Classic Corn' poop— makes
you wonder if you had corn, that you most
likely forgot,
And the 'Praying Naked' poop— that hurts so
bad, you're sweating and praying for it to
stop.

You must of heard of the 'Fart' poop, it's
also called a 'Shart'— it leaves your
underwear with a brown streak,
And last but not least, the 'Colon Express
poop, that leaves your butt so fast, when it
splashes, you end up with at least one wet
butt cheek.
We needed new names for Sam, Hank, Pete
and Tim to make the plan complete.

And Mitch was right, Carl accomplished the feat.
So he came up with 'Ticklish Tim', 'Hank The Stank', 'Snot Nose Sam', and 'Pimple Popping Pete'.

Stick Figure Stanley came up to us the next day before the school bell was about to ring,
With a book filled with drawings, since he can draw just about anything.
Any new information, or concept the teacher would bring,
To learn it, he drew it, and said to his brain it would cling.

Stick told us how he drew a PEMDAS chart to remember the order of operations.
In social studies, he drew a map for every ancient civilization.
In science, he drew the scientific method used for experimentation.
Even in ELA, he drew a plot chart to understand a story's creation.
He said he also drew other things, too, that had nothing to do with education.
Stuff he didn't understand, and everyday observations.

185

Like, why do desks get smaller as your grade
level goes up, what's the justification?
 So he drew a huge 12th grade kid sitting at a
toddler's desk, as an exaggeration.
This isn't what we asked him to do, what's the
correlation?
Whole time I'm wondering, what's the reason
for the procrastination?
Showed us another drawing, and I was like,
"You drew that, too? Wow, the imagination."
The school had a slight rodent infestation,
so he drew a rat with his own desk working on
a math calculation.
He drew Vanswoon flying on her broom stick,
over some urban location.
Made Dozer's hairpiece look like a crow that's
ready to fly to a new destination.
*Oh no, he didn't!*
He drew a pic of dead squirrel on a man's top
lip, and he said, "Hurst's mustache was the
inspiration."

Mitch asked him, "Were you in a drawing
contest but got disqualified?"
Stick said, "Not quite, some buster copied my
idea and lied.

He told the freaking judges I'm the one who
copied, and to my drawing it was applied.
I was like, really? Ya'll going to believe this
fool, who flip-flops like he's Jekyll and Hyde?
Who couldn't come up with nothing to draw,
then cried?
Whose breath smelled like something crawled
in his mouth and died?
He's just mad because when he asked to see
my drawing, I denied.
Thought of showing some proof, but forget
that— I got too much pride!
Since I didn't even bother to challenge it, my
guilt was implied."
Mitch just stared at him with those eyes
that were three inches wide.
"If I ever enter a contest again, it won't be
here at this school if I decide.
I don't care if the prize is a hundred dollar—
I rather shovel dog crap on the concrete
that's dried,
Or dress up as Jason Voorhees' Mom and wait
in the woods for him to arrive—
Or be stuck in Hank's crack and see how long
I'll survive—
Or to a grizzly bear who needs anger
management be tied—

187

Or sharing a suite with a skunk and his bride.
And for a while I tried to keep it on the low,
and wouldn't show my artistic side."

"Show us the wanted posters," Mitch began asserting.
All this anticipation and Stick's contemplation is so unnerving.
Hesitantly flipped to the back of his sketch book as if something's concerning.
He said, "I exaggerated some things, but you'll know to whom it's referring.
And we'll place them throughout the school building when no one is stirring.
In the bathrooms, while number ones and twos are occurring.
Even in class, while the cheat sheets and notes are swirling."
Mitch interrupted and was like, "Ok, we're still waiting." His impatience is surging,
He said he had a little trouble at first, not much effort he was exerting.
"I wasn't sure if I could make them harsh without your urging."
What's the point in all this, seems like around the truth he's circling.

"I even got stuck, and broke some pencils and markers and started cursing.

At first, I exaggerated the wrong features, some of my ideas weren't working.

And for a moment, back to a chump I felt like reverting."

*Uh oh! Where's he going with this...* "speed this up," I felt like blurting.

Said he had no choice but to think back to all the hurting.

"I desperately tried some other ideas and did some more researching.

Did my best to keep the focus on thoughts that need purging,

And finally made the wanted poster much more disturbing."


Tim was the first drawing he did;

It didn't even look like a kid.

It looked like something that used to be human, but was cursed and became something we hid.


At the top of the poster, it said "Ticklish Tim."

The chain was much too big for his neck that was thin...

189

Like the ankle of a flamingo.
His eyes were red like the chips used to play
Checkers or Bingo.

He drew a chest tattoo that said, "I need to
go to the gym,"
Because he can barely do one pull-up all the
way up to his chin.
Made his eyelids droop like old pillow cases,
and eyebrows were thin like dental floss on
him.

He made him extra skinny, too,— arms and
legs look like dry spaghetti sticks,
As if he weighed less than two baby chicks,
Or two mosquitoes, or possibly two ticks.
Lighter than loose change or a waiter's tips,
Or an extra small bag of potato chips.
Maybe two tear drop drips,
Or a couple of toothpicks,
Or perhaps a bad experiment that not even
Jesus can fix.

# Wanted

## With or without bugs

### Ticklish Tim

## $Reward

Dirty Baseball cap= $1.50
Fake Chain= $3.00

## For...

- Scaring children after dark
- Impersonating an insect
- Stealing the neighbors tires and using them for lips
- Using a boomerang for a neck
- Illegally housing bugs in his hair
- Wearing a fake chain and saying it's real
- Misusing the bags under his eyes to carry his life's savings

Next, was a drawing of 'Snot-Nose Sam'.
Whoever thought he was cool, this poster
proves it's a sham.
Made him look like a human potato— well
really, more like a yam.
Made his head the size of an astronaut's
helmet that students can't crop on their
smartphone's cam.
Drew him in a droptop Grand Am
Because his head wouldn't fit in a regular
sedan.
Or in any room with a ceiling fan—
Or in the machine they put you through to
get a CAT scan.
He'd probably tip over a minivan;
On the beach he probably blocks the sun
from those who are trying to get a tan.
He'd probably leave stretch marks on a
headband,
And it would be too heavy to float, if he
swam.
Made his nose look like two butt cheeks, or
baby hams—
Or like his nose was backed into by a Mack
truck and rammed.
Or as if to try to fit his face, it was
crammed,

And his nostrils look like two tunnels backed up like traffic jams.

Made his snot look like a polluted river dripping from a busted dam.

When I first saw it, my thoughts were, "You got a booty nose fam,"

Or, "OMG, someone get a plastic surgeon for your mans!"

His big teeth looked like dirty seashells and clams.

The space between them were deleted like unwanted emails or spam.

And eyes popped out of his head— you know, like as if his fingers were slammed.

# Wanted

**Snot Nose Sam**

**$Reward**

$Free box of tissues

DO I HAVE SOMETHING IN MY NOSE?

CORN ON THE COB DOESN'T STAND A CHANCE AGAINST THESE!

**FOR...**

-LOOKING LIKE AN EASTER EGG WHEN IT'S NOT EVEN EASTER.
-AVOIDING THE DENTIST HIS WHOLE LIFE.
-FALSELY USING BROKEN GLASS AS TEETH.
-SINGLE HANDEDLY SAVING TISSUE COMPANIES FROM BANKRUPCY.
-STEALING GOLF BALLS AND USING THEM FOR EYES.

The drawing of Hank was a hilarious work of art.
From his armpits, feet, and breath— he drew fumes to show a symphony of farts.
Drew his foot fat that made his sneakers spread apart,
Exposing his big toe, and made it look like another bully, Napoleon Bonaparte.
It was so thick it pulsated like a beating heart.
He had no neck, couldn't see where his chin ends and where his shoulders start.
Showed he had Twinkies, Yoohoos and Honey Buns, 'a la carte.
Had his failing grades hanging out his pocket, to show he's not smart.

Stuffed his fanny pack, and his belt didn't fit.
Made his mohawk look like a pSartan helmet.
Instead of hair, it looked more like velvet,
as if he gelled it.

He drew two man-boobs that looked like two levee sand sacks,
And a triple chin that resembled a pancake stack;

Made his belly button a crater on the moon, or an earthquake crack;
Made his ankle fat a little bully, pushing his socks back.

The last drawing was of 'Popping Pimple Pete'.
Drew him with his eyes flipped like a *Walking Dead* freak.
Gave him a huge veiny, steroid, muscle-bound physique.
Made his pimples look like small volcanoes exploding all over his cheek,


And it appears that from a dermatologist he fled,
With an extra-tight muscle-shirt, and 'Baby Gap' is what it said.
His baby brother probably tried to take his shirt back, but Pete sped.
He's probably a large, but he wore a smedium instead,
And hanging on for dear life— is each thread.
Someone must have told him the spandex fit is cool, but he was definately misled.
If he breathes in too deep, he'll probably rip the shirt— which he'll dread,
He made his unibrow look like an eagle landed on his forehead,
But now I'm thinking— it must be dead—
Because it just laid there with both wings spread.

Even his neck had a bicep, because his Adam's apple poked through.
He drew a custom grizzly bear carpet on his shoulders and chest, too.
That looked like a chest toupee from the pet zoo,
Or pieces of a fake mink coat that are attached with glue.
And it looked fluffy, too, like he used extra-bounce shampoo.

# For...

- STEALING SIZE "SMEDIUM" FROM BABY GAP.
- STEALING ANTHONY DAVIS' UNIBROW.
- GLUING HIS MOTHER'S WIG ON HIS CHEST.
- SHOVING TENNIS BALLS IN HIS BICEPS.
- MIXING TESTOSTERONE PILLS WITH HIS PROTEIN SHAKE.

Then, it was Fernando Flakes' chance to do his thing.

He said he wasn't always a dancer, but all that changed last spring.

There was an incident at the school dance that left a sting.

He said he showed up and people kept yanking him to the dance floor like a yo-yo string.

I said, "Did you know how to dance?" Flakes said, "Never!—

Not even Salsa, Bachata Merengue, or whatever."

Said he tried to do a dance he saw on one of his mother's favorite 'novelas'.

Said he was awful, and of the "no-rhythm" club he was a member.

"Everyone laughed; it was a day I'll always remember.

And they threw paper balls, paper cups till I surrendered.

I'm the only Puerto Rican in my family who wasn't a dancer."

He said he vowed never again to have no dance moves while on the dance floor's center.

And that he practiced all summer to get ready for September.

Mitch said, "Ok, hurry up and show us these dances for goodness' sake."
Then Flakes did some dances to a song by Drake.
He looked like a hot mess, or an uncoordinated mistake.
A weird arrangement of contortions that would make my body ache.

Now, to physically intimidate those bullies isn't easy, not one bit.
I've never had a real fight, this I'll admit.
Some of us probably have never thrown a punch— we're the ones that get hit.
They're so used to taking a loss, and some will even submit.
Plus these thugs are too much to handle together— to get them alone is the trick.
When Pete punched me in the stomach, I swear it felt like a brick.
Wish I was equipped with a Kung-Fu kick, or even a stick
'Cause if I swing, I'd probably look like a drunk chick.
Not to mention, the only one who could fight is Mitch.
I just heard him say, "Now it's time for the balance of power to switch."

# THE PAYBACK

## PART 2

### Chapter 14

Mitch had a plan for his old friendships to
suspend;

Split them up with slim hopes, to make amends.

He started spreading personal information
about his old friends,

And then, as if he had nothing to do with it, he
would pretend.

He told people about Sam's mother, who left
his father for a woman; that's what caused
the marriage to end,

But said it came from Tim— he typed it— then
hit send.

Told everyone Tim has a deadly disease, and
that his older sister Jenifer is easy, but she
goes by 'Jen'.-

And the word is... it came from Pete, whose
mouth leaks information every now and then.

Spoke about Hank's older brother, who has cerebral palsy, and beats him, not only on weekends;

That's why Hank is black and blue sometimes, 'cause it's not something he defends.

Mitch said Sam told us that, these Mitch lies we don't recommend.

He also told everyone that Pete is adopted, and by his real parents he was condemned.

Everyone thought Hank was the one who said it, then Pete went from zero to ten.

Mitch drew a wedge between each one of the bullies, so on each other, they could no longer depend.

Whatever happens next, I doubt they will comprehend.


As the next part of the plan evolved for us, we caught Hank after school, before he got on the bus.

It was me, Stick Figure, Flakes with Mitch, who told Hank they had something to discuss.

Stick Figure and Flakes started pushing and shoving Hank while their feet are kicking up dust.

Mitch paused and hesitated, as if he needed
to shake off some rust.
Then he tried to pick Hank up and struggled
with each hip thrust.

It was like picking up a rhino who's pregnant
with twins,
Or lifting a washer and dryer as it spins.

I tried to help by grabbing Hank by the neck,
and I scraped off his neck crust.
Every time Hank shifted his weight, my own
balance I couldn't trust.

It's as if I'm skating for the first time, with a
midget on my back—
My legs were about to give out, like I was
squatting a rack.

Hank dropped his weight on me and I felt my
spleen bust.
Knocked the wind out of me, breath came out
like a huge gust.

It felt like an elephant with butt implants sat
on me,

Or like I'm a bouncy house and too many kids are bouncing for free—
Or that there's a kangaroo on top of me jumping like it won the lottery.
Staring at me, because his pants are falling down, is meat from his butt.
We held Hank down, while grabbing his gut.
It felt like I was making pizza, grabbing and flipping dough,
Or playing with Play-Doh, or shaping mud on the low.

Snacks kept falling out of his fanny pack, and all he could say is, "My stuff!"
Hank's stench hit us in the nose like a wrench, and the other's faces were filled with disgust—

As if someone used the bathroom and didn't wash their hands and split,
Or while you're eating your favorite food, someone's spit lands in it.

I desperately avoided his armpits that reeked of musk.
Whole time I'm thinking, he'll think twice now before he insults.
Maybe do a double take and think about his own faults.                205

Look at the pros and cons and remember these assaults.
His belly rolls are moist and sticky as if he was dipped in puss.
Stick tried to cover Hank's mouth, because he is loud and couldn't help but cuss.
Out of shape and out of breath, Hank did his best to fuss.
They pressed their forearms against his man boobs, amidst his huffs and puffs.

Sounding like a lion with laryngitis,
As if he's suffering from appendicitis.

It was like wrestling with a mattress, and it was tough.
At times, it was like slow dancing with a girl that's too buff—

Or tangled up with a couch that smelled like a dirty sock—
Or having a beanbag in a head lock.

Hank kept screaming at us and saying, "Enough."
But if he wasn't so big, we wouldn't have to be so rough.

206

If he wasn't the size of a Mini Cooper,
And if his waistline didn't have a past, present and future.

We tried to hold our breaths, too, since by his smell, we were engulfed.
Dressed him in food jewelry and all kinds of foolery plus—
Threw on him a popcorn bracelet and a necklace, made out of peanuts.
Smeared on him ketchup and mustard, like makeup,
And put a coconut bra on his C-cups.
Shoved in each nostril a couple of slices of cold cuts,
And stayed on the lookout for any potential adult.

Put whipped cream on his eyebrows and his mohawk;
Put french fries down his mouth, and he couldn't talk.
Shoved him in a garbage can since he smelled like a garbage truck.
Hank was grabbing and pulling to get out, but he was stuck.
All the struggling back and forth, on the edge of the can, I got cut.

And on top of that, I think Hank sharted...
YUCK!
Mitch took a picture, on this day, Hank was straight out of luck
Never knowing what's going to happen; with paranoia he's struck.

Sam always goes to the bathroom at the end of fourth period to take a dump.
I was so nervous, my heart thumped,

As if I just got home and Mama is holding my report card,
Or like I'm giving a presentation in class, which is so hard.

It's like getting called to the principal's
office and not knowing what I did,
Or trying to talk to a girl for the first time,
God forbid.

We pushed Sam into the bathroom stall, and
you can tell, he got stumped.
Mitch gave him a shove, a push, and I gave
him a little bump.

He kept shoving us back, so we shoved him
even more.
We tried to avoid falling and landing on the
pissy bathroom floor.

It was like playing twister and being color—
blind, like bats,
Or playing Hopscotch— but on the ground
there's thumb tacks.

Tried to avoid his nose from dripping on the
clothes we wore,
From all the wrestling, I heard a sound like
someone's pants tore—
It sounded like a package being cut with a
box cutter from Pops' drawer.

This is the most physical activity I've had, I know tomorrow I'll be sore.


Tried to force Sam to sit on the toilet seat, no time to wait,
He kept forcing himself up, he refused to accommodate;
It was like forcing someone who's cockeyed to look straight,
Or like covering your food on a windy day with a paper plate.
He head-butted Stick in his bird chest to retaliate—
Mitch grabbed him from behind— but just a little too late.
Stick and Flakes are on each side, and I'm on his lap hoping to add the proper weight.


We duct-taped Sam to the toilet bowl, and the toilet bowl to his rump,
Then placed a sombrero on his head that's always plump.
He is slouched over, and his back made a slight hump.
He kept struggling and saying, "I ain't no chump!"

He threw a tantrum and tried to kick us, as if he knew karate.

He missed and instead kicked the stall wall, because his aim is spotty.

He kept growling at us like the engine on a Ferrari,

Or two dogs arguing over a T-bone steak in the lobby.

Sam was pissed; his face turned bright red and blotchy.

He trembled all over, from his inflated head to his body.

Either I was watching Bruce Banner right before he turns into that Hulk thing,

Or he's been bitten by a vampire and this is when he starts turning.

He kept frowning, refusing to show those teeth that looked like he played hockey.

I could see he was scared, and no longer cocky.

We stuffed Kleenex in his nose, because it was extra snotty.

The air from his gun barrel nostrils made my glasses a little foggy.

We put a sign around his neck that said "Snotty on the Potty"

Hanging from a string on a piece of
cardboard, that's beat up and shoddy.
Mitch texted the pic to the others, and Sam
didn't realize we each have a copy.

Next, we ran up on Tim to fool.
He likes to hang and shoot around in the gym
after school.

Snuck up on Tim...and he said, "I know ya'll
not finna sneak up on me."

Tim threw the basketball and hit Stick in the knee.

We grabbed him and he said, "I know I'm not finna get grabbed by you three."

He's so skinny, he slipped through with a shimmy

And said, "I know ya'll not finna let me be this slippery."

Stick grabbed his shirt and ripped his white tee.

Again he said, "I know ya'll not finna rip my shirt like it's free."

Then Tim punched Flakes on the nose and he couldn't see.

While saying, "I know ya'll finna let me be."


Mitch tackled him with a shoulder to the mid-section,

The way a receiver tackles a cornerback after an interception.

Tim landed on the hardwood, bones bouncing with no protection.

He bit Mitch on the shoulder with a sudden aggression,

As if it was "Man Meat Mondays" and Mitch is his selection.

He fluttered some kicks at me and 'Sticks direction,
Like he was pedaling a bike in midair, is the perception—
Or trying to float in a pool after only one swimming lesson.
We eventually grabbed both legs, but Flakes was the exception.
He is mostly the look out, and his focus is adult detection.
We took his shirt and pants off, but left his boxers on, revealing his imperfections.
His belly button was so big, it's like they placed a clown nose there without his blessing;
And a goatee underneath it, that's so thick, you can use a hair pick to pick it, I'm guessing.
Poured syrup all over his body ignoring his objections,
Kept saying "I'm allergic to sweets, no exceptions!
Can I get sugar diabetes from this?" was his ridiculous question,
Looking like a cinnamon pretzel stick at the mall's concessions.
We dumped two bags of feathers all over his body at Mitch's discretion,

214

As if he's part of a Perdue inspection,
Or some type of Bird Man resurrection.

Tim is upset, what did he expect?
If you hurt others, you get hurt back— cause
and effect.
Then we took a pic of our latest project.
Now Tim knows what it feels like to be a
rejected object.
He probably has never felt so low, I bet,
But if he thought this was the worst of it—
no, not yet.

Now we're down to Pete, the biggest pain we searched for all afternoon.
We almost quit looking, but decided to resume.
We checked the gym lockers and heard something go— BOOM!
What do you know— Pete was knocked out sleeping in back of the locker room!
He just laid there exposing his armpits that looked like the Bristles of a broom.

Looking like he had two raccoons in a headlock,
Or like he's a retailer and he's got armpit weaves in stock.

But he ain't gotta be this hairy; to shaving he must be immune.
He should at least consider using a pair of hedge trimmers to prune.
He was even snoring— wind from his nostrils was like a monsoon.
The only other sound we heard was a radio in Wiffersnuv's office playing an old-school tune.
We propped him up against the lockers, with his eyes closed; he no longer looks like a goon.

He no longer looks like that dude that gets a full blown workout squeezing pimples and moles.
You know, that Pete guy, who's the definition of an internet troll.


We cut a hole in the pizza box, placed it over his head that stuck out like a balloon.
Placed a pepperoni on every other pimple, that looked like little red moons,
While in deep sleep he seemed to be consumed.
Then, we sprinkled in some olives, peppers and mushrooms.
We tried to hurry, thought he'd wake up soon.
We did what we had to do, not worried of which consequences would loom.
On his forehead we wrote "pizza face" since he wore a pizza box as a costume.
That's it! We took the last pic and he looked like a buffoon!
He's going to try to kill us from now till the end of June!

The next day Myrtle came up to us, who can write rhymes and songs in English, Spanish and Greek.

Not only is she on the Debate Team, but she's in a school concert every couple of weeks.

She also knows how to play the piano, while wearing the gloves, and ignoring the critiques.

We asked Myrtle if she was able to do some of these things, even before she could speak.

She said, "I don't know, but how my teacher found out was so embarrassing, that I almost freaked.

I liked this boy in class, so I wrote him a poem about how much I liked his eyes, his hair, even his physique.
Gave it to one of his friends to pass to him, and this is where the story begins to reek.
Before it made it to his friend, the poem circulated through everyone's hand on the sneak.
When the boy finally got it, his laughter made my misery peak.
Then things took a turn for the worse, and my teacher intercepted it and took a peek.
She read a couple of lines out loud in front of the whole class, as if more attention I was trying to seek."
After a pause, she continued, "And it felt like a kick in my lower oblique.
At first my teacher couldn't believe that with words, I had so much technique.
She apologized for embarrassing me, then made me a full-fledged Band Geek."
Then I asked her, "So, can we hear these rhymes about these bullies for everyone to repeat?"

Myrtle said she tried to write a song, but had trouble finding a melody.

Every tune she hummed was wrong, as she tried to find a remedy.
Then it dawned on her— all she has to do is write a parody!
She said she'd be stealing someone else's melody, but it's not a real felony.
It has to be something popular, a song we'll never forget.
Something that was on the billboards forever, and millions of downloads were received on the net.

The first parody was to the melody of a song by Far East Movement called, "Like a G6"—
To take jabs at Pete, instead she said, "Pete's pimples pop like a cheese stick."

The next parody uses the melody of the song "Bad and Boujee" by Migos;
Instead she called it "Slimy Boogies" and it's about Sam and why he's gross.
The next parody was of Ticklish Tim and it was funny times three.
She wrote it to the melody of, "Bodak Yellow" by Cardi B.

The last parody was of Hank— to finish her part of the plan.

220

It was to the melody of, "Shape of You," by
Ed Sheeran.
Renamed it "Taste of Food" since of food
he's a number one fan.

The same day, Matt rolled up on us avoiding a
few spills.
This is how everyone found out that he had
skills.
He said he got sick of seeing these bullies
hurt others for thrills,

So he hacked the school's grading system,
like he was CIA.
Changed the bullies grades to Fs, but it's not
like they had As and Bs anyway.
"I didn't think they would even check, they
barely go to class, okay.
And the teachers were confused once they
heard what the parents had to say.
The principal found out, and I got an in-
school suspension for a day."

Mitch said Matt is like some software
programmer and internet sage,
because he created a fake Instagram and
Snapchat page—

Designed to get every kid in the school engaged;
Boy or girl, it didn't matter what age.

Matt was glad he had the chance to do something that was way overdue.
He called it "Bully Beatdown", a name that quickly grew.
He posted the pictures we took, and the wanted posters Stanley drew.
And with those pics, he created memes to spread, like the flu.
Some things were exaggerated, some things were true.
Identities won't be mistaken, our message people won't misconstrue.
A lot of them were things, most of us already knew,
Designed to get 'likes' and 'follows' and many people to view.
As soon as it's posted, let's see if the roasting will ensue.
Also, he created links and threads to be sent to a list of student emails, too.
It took some time for everything to go through.

When you ask Domino's to give you the pizza for free, since they took longer than 30 minutes.

WHEN YOUR MOTHER SAYS, "THROW EVERYTHING THAT SMELLS IN THE

Me= I'm not afraid of nothing!
Also me....

Me

On Taco Tuesdays!

What's going to follow— I don't have the slightest clue!
I asked Mitch, "How did you find out what Suszie can do?"
Apparently, she had started a GoFundMe for people to donate to;
To raise money for bulimia, a disease that affects... ummm... I'm not sure who.
He said, "Everyone knows, I guess everyone— but you!
She spread the word through social media for everyone to view.
She posted it on Snap, Instagram, and on Facebook, too.
It spread like wild fire, and word around town grew.
It spread like a virus, or some kind of bird flu.
Heard she raised like thousands of dollars by week two.

And now it's her chance to do what she does best;
Using social media to gossip and also through text,
Using her own page to promote and suggest,
The "Bully Beatdown" Instagram and Snapchat to add, follow, or request.

Mitch said, "She was texting the pics and links with a full court press.

Even the bullies' personal information is expressed.

She even spread it through word of mouth— single-handedly— I'm impressed.

She's usually annoying and considered a pest,

But this time, what's she's yapping about, they didn't detest.

It appears that gossiping is how she's blessed.

She was in the zone, she even looked obsessed.

That much talking in such little time would've had anybody else stressed.

Heard about it in the locker room while we got dressed.

People spoke about it in class, even passed notes during a test.

They spoke about it in the Caf while waiting for their food to digest.

I would hear things like, "Did you see it?...Yes!"

And, "Oh my God, they're a mess."

"It's so embarrassing... I guess."

Someone else said, "I laughed so hard, I felt some pain in my chest."

This was the talk of the town for a week, no contest.

# BULLY BREAKDOWN

## Chapter 15

For the next couple of days, everything was on a roll.

Every time someone saw a wanted poster, or got a text, they would lose control.

Snickering and laughing in the bullies' faces, straight up bold.

Some would repeat the rhymes Myrtle wrote, as if it were R&B to the soul.

They did Fernando's dances, like they were listening to Rock & Roll,

And those pics we took, fulfilled their goal.

Stanley's drawings were on the lockers and flag pole.

Some couldn't believe what they heard, no matter how they were told.

Some expressed that the rumors were ice cold.

Many commented on the social media posts, like an internet troll.

Though the posts were in English, some responded in Espanyol.                226

They kept sharing the fake profiles that
Matt hacked or stole.
There are so many likes and followers, even
an online poll...
For instance:
Who's likely to wear a waist trainer
underneath their clothes...
Who's likely to go see a plumber to fix a leak
in their nose...
Who's likely to make out with a cheeseburger
and propose...

Who's likely to jump through a straw and not
touch the sides...
Who's likely to take a deep breath and we see
their insides...
Who's likely not to be seen, if behind a Q-tip
he hides...

Who's likely to get a recipe tattooed on their
belly...
Who's likely to cause two flat tires when
riding in a Chevy...

Who's likely to be mistaken for a whale at the
beach...
Who's likely to be embarrassed for toes they
can't reach...                          227

Who's likely to get caught with a protein bar they stole...
Who's likely to use monopoly money to pay a toll.
Who's likely to smell like a baboon's butthole...
The choices are Sam, Hank, Pete and Tim- listed left to right— as you scroll.


There were first account eyewitnesses of each ordeal.
It started first thing in the morning, here's the deal.
Pete was walking in the hallway and the scabs from his popped pimples he would peel.
Passed two girls that sounded like a dolphin arguing with a seal—
Arguing over pretty boy Shawn— who they're both trying to steal.
He probably doesn't like either one of them, but he got that kind of appeal.
All of a sudden, Pete saw the drawing that made him look like a heel—
Right there on his locker-and he banged his fist against the steel!
Snapped and grabbed some kid in the hallway by the collar who wore a shirt the color of teal.

Angrily asked him, "Who drew this?" But the kid stuttered and had nothing to reveal.

Mr. Charles came around the corner and said, "Boy get your hands off!"
Voice all raspy, choking on phlegm as he coughed.
He continued, "Grab someone your own size, this kid might as well be a tall dwarf."
Maybe deep down inside, Pete is a little soft.
But into a monster Pete continued to morph,
Like King Kong after seeing Jane run off.

Suddenly, he ripped the wanted poster down and balled it in his hand, so it's concealed.
Then used his phone to check and see if the information on the poster is for real.
He stormed off and belted a roar, like a cougar who just lost its meal—
Or a bear who got a thorn stuck in its heel-
Or better yet a bull who got his horns stuck, which wouldn't be ideal.
He ended up crashing into a girl selling tickets for the dance, like a drunk driving an automobile.
The tickets flew up in the air like confetti;
Like graduation caps coming down real steady.

Some flew to the side, the way a car after a crash loses its wheel.
Pete hasn't been to school since then, so you could probably figure out how he must feel.

Hank found out when he was in the caf,
Always sitting with two trays of food and he already ate half.
You can smell the aroma of the food being made by the lunch staff.
A couple of girls passed by pointing to Hank's calf;
One had a neck long enough to compete with a giraffe.
A couple more walked by and they laughed.
You could feel the chill in the air and it wasn't a draft.

Three boys came over with a small paper ball stack
To shoot free throws in Hank's butt crack.
They are supposedly "Band Geeks"; one was named Jack;
They shot a couple but missed; Hank didn't even react.
Hank was devouring a slice of pizza, you can hear his lips smack.

He's committed to finishing, as if he signed a contract—
Or took an oath to stay fat.
It appears they weren't afraid anymore of Hank's bully attack.
It seems like anyone can get it now, others also want payback.
All this karma Hank didn't expect; it's what he now apparently attracts.
There's a look on his face, as if he's ready to crack,
Or waiting for a UFO, for his body to extract.

Now his fists are balled up; guess he's feeling the impact.
I began to worry about what he planned to do, and that's a fact.
I even called out his name, the plan was to distract.
Hank got curious to see what they were laughing at;
Got up quicker than he usually does, fanny pack intact.

Shoved a girl and her phone, he straight snatched.

231

He saw the pics and drawings in a folder
batched.
This must be why kids were targeting him; he
must have felt unmatched.
One kid lifted Hank's shirt and said, "Guess
the baby in your stomach hasn't hatched."
Another hung an air freshener, to Hank's
shirt it was attached,
And placed a bunch of stickers on Hank's
back, the kind that smell when scratched.
From that moment on, from everyone, Hank
was completely detached.

Sam realized what happened, while sitting in
Mr. Dozer's class.
He noticed notes and phones from hand-to-
hand pass.
Some tried to keep it on the low, and didn't
put it on blast.
Whispers from row to row— but he was the
one to know last.

One kid kept picking his nose with every
finger, even his thumb.
Thinks we don't see him, then on the floor he
flicks some.

Wipes it on his leg, and smears it underneath
the desk next to the chewed gum.
They refused to pass him anything— yeah,
he's another gross one.


From a distance, Sam recognized a pic from
this boy's phone;
It was the pic from when he got jumped in the
bathroom alone.


They passed around the wanted poster,
crumbled up in their hands like trash.
Sam intercepted it, then opened and ripped it
up in a flash.
Meanwhile, Pretty Boy Shawn is winking and
showing off a hand full of cash.
He's blowing kisses to this girl, and his lips are
white like ash.
The girl behind him got pissed; the other
girl's face she is ready to bash.
Shawn has that magic that makes all the girls
clash.


From left to right, they threw tissue at Sam
for his nose that's never blown.
Heard this boy drew a face on a balloon that
he blew up on his own.

233

Passed it around while the teacher wasn't looking, and called it a "Snot Nose Sam clone". When Sam saw it, he grabbed and popped it; much anger was shown.

Girls were startled; the teacher said, "What was that?" In a terrified tone.

Every time Dozer turns around, his hair piece moves, as if it's not sewn.

Looked like a dead animal that had once flown.

Everyone gladly pointed to Sam; in his direction, blame was thrown.

Sent his own self to the principal's office, like he was grown.

As he left the class, he heard "Snotty on the potty" with some grunts and moans,

As if they're dropping a load on the porcelain throne.

Heard he never made it to the office, and since then his whereabouts are unknown.

Tim found out when he went to use the bathroom.

The wanted posters were taped all over the walls looking like a cartoon.

Heard someone was in the stall doing number two, judging by the fumes.

Someone else tried to come in, but did a one—
eighty, because it smelled like burnt prunes.
The memes were printed and also hung up; too
much for Tim to consume.
Staring at them were two older boys, one of
whom,
Pointed and laughed, stopped and saw Tim,
then resumed.
Tim yelled, "Shut up!" and charged the wall like
a platoon.

Tore down everything on the wall, in full rage—
The posters, the memes, every single page;
Like a psychotic released from a cell, or animal
sprung from a cage.
A horrifying, yet dramatic performance, if this
were a stage.

While he did that, one of the boys recited the
rhymes Myrtle wrote about Tim.
One said, "It's Ticklish Tim, you ain't smiling,
where's that stupid grin?"
The other did Fernando's dances, while
swinging each limb.
Another had a water bottle and said, "Here's
some water, heard chickens can't swim."
Opened the water bottle and threw water on
him;

Heard Tim walked away with watery eyes and a vibe that's now grim,
Like he was scorned or something was being torn from within.
Heard after that, Tim walked around and hid his face underneath his hat's brim.
Never saw him after school anymore, playing ball in the gym,
And the annoying smirk he wore has now been dimmed.

We used to feel humiliated, but that has now faded.
No more feeling upset, or being a reject that's jaded.
We finally navigated these feelings of hatred.
"We ain't getting bullied no more", our actions stated.
We're just trying to survive, so our lives aren't negated.
At what we just pulled off, even that weird kid in the hallway with no emotions was elated.
We chanted, "Payback is a b%$&!"— as we celebrated.
They hit us with the PG-13, but the payback was R-rated.

236

We would get an 'A' for a@# kicking if we were graded.

They thought they built a fortress, but it's been invaded.

We did nothing for so long, I'm glad we waited.

I disagreed at first with Mitch, I'm glad I was persuaded.

We are a great team, I'm glad the others aided.

All these bully egos are no longer inflated.

They are hard to find now, seems like school grounds have been vacated.

We're still laughing at Tim, who was degraded,

And with ketchup and mustard, Hank's face we painted—

And those hilarious 'Wanted Posters' Stanley created.


We all cheered and I had an awkward high-five with Stick.

Told Carl to give me five, and he took a five dollar bill out of his pocket, quick.

He must be used to having his money taken, 'cause at first I didn't get it.

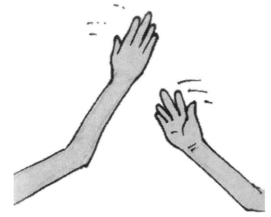

I even tried to give him a pound, but he flinched;
He must have thought he was going to get punched when he saw my fist was clinched.

Stick went too high with his high-five, as if a pitcher throwing a pitch,
And I went too low, as if my elbow was caught on a hitch.

238

Mitch said, "That's the most fun I've had, I really hope they don't snitch."
Then turned to me and said, "I'm glad you switched."

Mitch and Stick did a chest bump.
Stick is so skinny, he landed right on his rump.
Matt tried to pop a wheelie, since he can't jump.
But he had a little trouble— in the way was a tree stump!
Stick concluded, "Don't look now guys, but I'm no longer a chump!"

Stick Figure said, "I'm glad the posters worked.
Yeah! No more notes on the back of my shirt."

Suzie said, "Too bad this wasn't something that could've been resolved with just talk."
Then to celebrate, Fernando pop-locked into a handshake and a moonwalk.
Suzie and Myrtle played patty-cake to celebrate, and it was a disgrace;
Both girls are uncoordinated; they accidentally slapped each other in the face!

Carl was jumping up and down, as if he'd won the lottery,

And almost poked our eyes out with his long nose, without an apology.

Carl said, "The nicknames he gave to them were quality—

But the rhymes that Myrtle wrote were pure comedy!

Carl proposed, "I'm never getting shoved in a locker again, no one will bother me."

Meanwhile, Suzie's sharp scream of excitement could've broken some pottery.

She speculated, "No more fake bugs"; she can now eat in peace foods that will probably block every artery.

Myrtle is clapping with her gloves on as usual, applauding our camaraderie.

Ink in her soda can, she no longer has to worry.

She turned to Suzie and said, "How you gossip is a real commodity."

Then suggested to me, "Wear something nice afterwards for the party."


Once our high died down, we were done with our celebrations.

We all went our separate ways, no clue of their destinations.

I stayed behind by the bleachers, reflecting on some observations.
The abilities we have, that get no appreciation.
We thought we were losers, and were blinded by our limitations,
But we all have something we can do, all kinds of unique qualifications.
Some of us can draw amazing illustrations;
We're all special and have our own aspirations.
Despite these stereotypes and generalizations,
There's always a way to fight— we learned through this collaboration.
I remember Mama told me: "Here's how you handle a bully situation.
There's no talking, no pleading, no type of negotiation.
Because sometimes, words are subject to misinterpretation.
There's no running like you're in a Doberman chase simulation;
No seeking peace with meditation.
You can engage the bully in physical altercation,
But if you're too weak or can't fight, here's another recommendation:

Take some self-defense classes, and avoid the
initiations—
Or try some wise cracks, some insults, or joke
combination.
No one messes with the funny kid, because
that comes with some humiliation.
Either you beat them up, or embarrass them,
no need for an explanation."


For the rest of the week, everyone treated us
different;
I wasn't treated like an illegal immigrant.
It seems we're looked upon now, as more
equivalent.
Guess we curved thoughts that are ignorant;
Too bad it took such an unforeseen
predicament.
Here comes Mr. Charles again, who's now even
more vigilant.


Walking towards me with his fist up,
declaring, "Fight the power!"
Smelling like cheap cologne and cigars— boy
he needs another shower!
People giving me a thumbs-up or a high five—
at least one every hour.

I'm even getting chat message requests popping up on my browser.
I'm also getting compliments now, no more words that are sour,
Saying they like my bow tie, "Is that paisley or flowers?"
Carl is wearing jeans now, no more trousers.
Even Stick is dripping with swagger now, looking prouder.
While Myrtle walks with her black gloves on, looking like a prowler.
Walking with her head high, as if no one will clown her.
Walking with confidence now, I don't have to cower.
We're the cool kids now, we silenced our doubters.
Girls smiling at me now, and in class I speak louder.
When sharing a textbook in class now, they say "ours".

I was feeling myself, then Mr. Dozer stopped me like a bouncer,
Spoke to me with the same voice of a radio announcer.

He stressed, "You're walking now, but at some point expect to flounder."

He must know something, 'cause he acts like a Debbie Downer.

He said, "What's lost is sometimes found in the dirt."

Pats me on the back.

*Is he implying we're gonna get hurt?*

*Is he trying to intervene?*
*He's speaking in riddles, what does he really mean?*

Then out of nowhere— with Simone I have an encounter.

She asks "if we can talk" and she's without the pack of slobbering wolves that usually surrounds her.

I didn't know what to say, so I just blurted, "What do you want?"

*Is she trying to set me up for another ruthless taunt?*

This is strange...all of a sudden, a smile she's willing to flaunt,

But I paid it no mind, played it cool and nonchalant.

We were right by the auditorium, in the
middle of the hallway.
Felt like everybody was watching, like I'm a
bridesmaid who just caught a bouquet.
My shirt is untucked, bow tie was crooked;
my look was in complete disarray.
Out of all the days she could have spoke to
me, of course she chose today.

With her Caribbean, Princess of Pop Rihanna-
like stance,
Wearing an outfit, Mama could never finance,
Simone asked, "Do you have any plans to go to
the dance?"
Her friend Heaven is with her, with that
huge butt that look enhanced.
For Myrtle's whereabouts, I took a paranoid
glance.
Also trying not to lose myself in those pretty
eyes and get stuck in a trance.
It didn't work; still slipped in a daydream
that involved me in some romance.
I lied and said I had no plans, then she made
an advance.
Next, she said something that made my
heartbeat prance;

Asked me to come with her, and to give it a chance.

My first thought is, what am I going to tell Myrtle?
I already promised her, getting out of it will be a hurdle.
Do I take the practical route, or the one that's more commercial?
Pondering what to do is taking too long, deciding is slower than a turtle.
Then felt a booger ready to bungee jump out of my nostril.
So I covered my nose, as if there's a smell that's hostile.
Myrtle has become a friend, even though she's controversial,
But Simone is the prettiest girl in school; I even wrote it in my journal.
She could have spared me from the park incident, but chose to be nonverbal.
And I still remember the pain, because it's mostly internal.
But if I bail out on Myrtle, wouldn't that be more hurtful?
All this back and forth my thoughts are going in a circle.

But I get it, I'm a cool kid now, went from a
private to a colonel.
Went from a desert to a land that's fertile—
Went from being Urkle, to Stefan or
Herschel—
Went from being a disease, to something
holistic, or herbal.
Wish I could have practiced for moments like
this— a Pretty Boy Shawn rehearsal;
Or had someone to teach me the ropes, but
no hopes of a mentor referral.
The awkward silence became eternal...
Gripped my fingers so tight, they started
turning purple.
I tried to think of an answer to give that's
vague, or universal.
Was about to say "ok" but did a reversal.
If I said "maybe", would that make it
official?
Even thought, for whom would this be
beneficial?
Then the words "I can't" shot out like a
missile.
The more I think about it, I realize she's
superficial.

## Chapter 16

Pete didn't come to school for a couple of
days, and Mrs. Vanswoon became concerned.
She said, "Homework has to be made up,
lessons have to be learned."
He's probably still trying to figure out how he
got burned,
Probably retracing the steps to see how the
tables were turned.
I'm sure he's not accepting any blame,
thinking these acts were never earned.
Mitch mentioned he knows Pete is furious but
he can't confirm;
Probably sitting somewhere, his thoughts
making his blood churn,
And that he's probably throwing things, like a
lover who's spurned.

Maybe he locked himself in his room doing
pushups and curls.

He must be lost without his favorite course—
harassing the girls...
I'm sure he misses pulling on their hair, that
with his finger he'd twirl,
Telling all the Black and Spanish ones "we
make a good swirl".

Not sure if he can make up all this work he
missed, he doesn't appear to be smart.
Someone told Mitch, "Instead of going to
school, Pete is hanging out at the park."
Mitch said to me, "A couple of things are
concerning, umm... where do I start?
Well... Pete had a book in his hand that he was
tearing apart,
And that he was beating on his chest— on the
left side— right by his heart.
When he sees someone from school, in a
second he'll dart.

Heard he was looking unkempt,
Like for at least a week he hasn't slept.
Heard someone called him "Petee Puss Puss,"
and he got really upset.
It was brisk, so, I'm sure the hairs on his back
must have leapt.

Heard he had his head down as if he wept,
As if he's feeling completely inept;
Guess being a loser is hard for him to accept.
He must be at the point where shame and pride intersect.
With his foot, back and forth the leaves he swept,
Dragging his heels and the tip of his toes, as he stepped.
Heard he was surprisingly quiet; on the squirrels he crept,
As if for something worse he contemplated, or prepped."


Sam eventually came back to school, but kept leaving class,
Hiding behind the staircase with a nurse pass.
Someone said they saw him crying in the hallway, behind the door's glass.
Heard he looks annoyed and doesn't want to be seen, so he walks fast.
Then he goes into the nurse's office ten minutes before the bell blasts,
Complaining about his asthma, as if his lungs are ready to collapse.
"What's the real problem, why are you in here everyday?" I'm sure the nurse asked.

He probably didn't respond, and changed the subject, perhaps.
He refuses to play gym outside now, as if he's allergic to grass.
He doesn't take his daily dump anymore, and we can certainly tell he still has gas.
In the way are these excruciating days he tries to outlast;
Heard he dropped out of the school play, even though it's for a small role he is cast.
We became aware that he complained to the principal about being harassed.

We heard Tim is walking around with disguises,
Like— who does he think he's fooling?
In class, he keeps his hoodie on; teacher asks, "What are you doing?"

He has his baseball cap pulled down to his eyes; all you see is brim.
When he wears his sweater, it's pulled up over his (elbow-like) chin.
Sometimes he puts sunglasses on, but we all know it's him.

One side of his head is in cornrows, the other side is an afro still; it's confusing.
Heard he tried to transfer to his cousin's school, but his mom said, "We ain't moving!"—
The same school a month ago where there was a shooting.
He's hanging out on the corner of the pawn shop, harmful things he must be choosing.
Talks under his breath, like he has nothing left, his mind he's losing.
Hear him mention pain, not sure what that meant, but says it's consuming.
Comes to school now smelling like smoke— he must be using.
Heard the counselor tried to offer him help, but he keeps refusing.
Reluctant to smile, and for a while— he found nothing amusing.
He's depressed, I'm assuming…

Heard his mother picks him up often,
Discovered it is because of a sickness— not sure if it's a lie, or a real precaution.

Hank appeared to have the hardest time dealing;

He must have felt more fat than ever, but that didn't stop him from feeding.
He scarfed down his lunch so fast, you can hear his food pleading.
He must be scarred by the butt-crack free throws, he doesn't bend down now; instead he's kneeling.
He wears a hoodie now to hide his man boobs, because his cropped jersey is too revealing.
He's getting bigger and bigger; when he sits down, you can hear the chair squeaking.
When he finally came to the cafe, he sat in the corner with cuts on his arms, and it seems as if he's bleeding...
He even had a rash and his skin is peeling.
Realized tragic novels and dark comic books he's now reading;
A solution to the shame and pain, he must be seeking.
His thoughts must be lost; not sure what he's believing.
His mood swings, everyone is now seeing.
He's quick to get agitated, and then there he goes... he's always leaving.
He's not saying much, but I'm sure inside he's screaming.

You wouldn't even know he was there, if it wasn't for the sound of a rhinoceros breathing;
When he does, he talks of revenge, but without saying whom he'll be defeating.
If he's not looking down, he's staring at the ceiling.
The guidance counselor and Hank's parents had a meeting,
About the depression and sadness Hank has been feeling...
Or maybe for doing no homework and classwork, and definitely overeating.
Heard he was lashing out; he got caught at the pharmacy for stealing.
I rarely see him on the bus anymore, he's probably still healing.
Perhaps he's still trying to avoid the verbal and physical beating.


Back in Vanswoon's class on a cold day in November chillin',
Like a serenading serpent— the heat from the heater kept hissing.
She kept stressing the importance of the next test, but I didn't need convincing.

She's flying around the class doing her witch
thing.
A couple of boys shaking their legs wondering
when will they be pissing,
Because Witch Vanswoon had a "no bathroom"
rule since the beginning.
Pete and Hank came to school today, guess
they're over the dissing.
Hate being in a class with Pretty Boy Shawn,
it seems like for something he's always
fishing.
Scouting for his latest victim with— "pssst...
hey, Ma"— he starts his pitching.
It's awkward to have Simone in my class now
with the sex appeal she's emitting.
As always, there are two boys in the back
playing a game of hitting.
Heaven is by the pencil sharpener, wedgie
digging,
As if inside her pancreas her underwear is
swimming.
Looked like she was pulling the stuffing out of
a turkey for Thanksgiving.
Once again, I was in the middle of
daydreaming and reminiscing;
Then I noticed a box cutter fell out of Pete's
pocket while he was sitting.

I did a quick double take— not sure if I was tripping,

Because I didn't see a box anywhere that needs shipping.

*What could he need that for?* In my mind, some possibilities I'm dismissing.

He picked it up suspiciously fast, so no one knew what he was getting.

He kept fussing with it, inside his pockets, he was clicking.

*Does he want someone to notice, is he tipping?*

His other hand is on top of the desk and I see it twitching.

He was mumbling  words to a song from prior listening;

Something about someone or something that won't be living,

And thanking God because after that, he'll need forgiving.

*Do I tell the teacher? Do I speak to him outside?* My conscious is insisting.

*Should I ask for the box cutter? Would he be resisting?*

*Do I tell Mitch, and we take it from him? Not sure if he'd be willing.*

*Should I pretend I saw nothing?* I'm not used to interfering.
*But if I do nothing, what am I risking?*
The more I think about it, I sense my heartbeat skipping.
This anxiety almost feels like my intestines are ripping.
Don't know what his intentions are, or what he plans on committing.
He cracks a slight smile now, a real sadistic type of grinning.
*Oh my God!...* I think there's someone he plans on killing.


Hank just walked out the class without saying a word, or getting a pass either.
Mysteriously disappeared like he was trying to escape the reaper.
And as far as Pete is concerned, I decided, I'm going to tell the teacher.
Oh no... really? Siren just goes off for a fire drill procedure.
We are rushed out, and Vanswoon is in front of the line, as our leader.
It's supposed to be silent, but many spoke like it was time for leisure.

Vanswoon is getting annoyed with the commotion, and I feel her.

We're all bumping along; you got your floppers and some who are weavers.

I kept my eyes on Pete, like I was stalking a rare creature.

While the girls keep their eyes on Shawn, I think they must sense he's a cheater.

Still no sign of Hank; I asked Mitch, he concurred, "Me neither."

You can't miss him... he takes up the same amount of space as an industrial freezer,

And you can smell him from afar; don't need to be a bloodhound or golden retriever.

When the crowd thickens, I try to find Pete by locating his sneakers.

Some of the students are by the front entrance, others in the back by the bleachers.

But the parking lot on the side of the school is where we were.

It's cold outside, but it feels like I have a fever.

Anticipating Pete's every move has me overheating like a busted heater.

Every time he puts his hand in his pocket, I almost have a seizure.
A hundred things flash in front of my eyes— and everything is mute, like an unplugged speaker.
What if Pete sees the one he wants to cut and gets too eager?
Should I tackle him, the way a cornerback does to a wide receiver?
False alarm— he takes his hand back out— oh boy, I need a breather!

There goes Tim, still with a hoodie on like he is spying.
With a dejected disposition, not sure if it's sweat, or tears he's wiping.
Hasn't said a word; by now he's usually rhyming.
I'm glad to see that he's surviving.
These bullies still don't speak to each other, guess they're not uniting.
There goes another siren—the sound of the fire drill retiring.
Everyone is walking back to the building, the commotion now is spiking.
As time passes, I can't help anticipating something soon is igniting.

Ohhh! I think I see Sam-a snot-nose sighting!
His head sticks out the crowd, not surprising,
Like a bobblehead in the middle of a midget uprising!
With a small hat on it, he should consider resizing.
The only one with a backpack on, like he's going camping or rock climbing.
Like a sprinter, he was striding,
But I don't think his intention is exercising.
Rushed to be first in the building, nervously looking behind him.


Maybe he's going to look for something he's having a hard time finding.
Didn't even care that his sneakers were untying.
His fingernails, he's constantly biting.
He's got my curiosity going, is there something he's hiding?
Then, he snuck into the bathroom...hmmm... suspicious timing.


 Like an undercover cop, I'm still on Pete's trail.
I'll circle back to Sam later, I have a stabbing to curtail.

Trying to stay close and at the same time distant, and whatever that may entail.

Pete walks slower than I do, so I slow my pace down to a snail.

He turned the corner; I bumped into a random female.

If I fell, he would know that I was following, so I held onto the rail.

I tried to calm myself with thoughts of me in a tall tale.

In my mind, I stopped the stabbing attempt, and saw my courage prevail.

Then back to reality, because those thoughts are of no avail.

*Should I jump in the way? Heck no! I'm too frail!*
*Maybe I can distract him, and show him muscle t-shirts on sale.*

Then he went inside the gym and blocked the doors with a scale.

*Oh no!! I'm going to get help! I gotta bail!*

Ran so fast in the hallway, the wind would hit me like a sail.

Also trying to get my story together, each and every detail.

Put my hand on my knees, took a break to inhale and exhale...

Back to running like my hair's on fire... it's too costly to fail...
*I need to hurry, someone might end up in the hospital or in jail!*

All this running around, I didn't see one adult.
I figured sooner or later, I'll run into someone but...
There goes the bathroom where Sam had snuck!
Slowly Cracked the door open, for once it was unstuck...
Stayed low like someone threw a blow, and I began to duck.
Sam was on the floor with a suspicious box and a lighter, which he struck.
He was intently focused like no one should disrupt.
He looked stressed like a volcano, ready to erupt.
*Is that a fuse he's trying to light? Yup!!*
I shut the door, dropped to the floor— I think he's trying to blow us up!

*I gotta get back up, pull it together, no excuse.*

There's a snot-nose bomber and a pimple face
stabber on the loose.
Seems like I'm running in circles, or in a sick
game of Duck, Duck Goose...
Paused in front of the auditorium, felt like a
heart attack was being induced!
My nerves are shot, the counselor would say
this is 'psychological abuse.'
This all would've been different, had we tried
to call a truce.
I could've never imagined this kind of pain our
actions could produce.
Looked inside the glass door, hoping someone
inside could be of use;
But all I see is Tim again, standing on a chair
on stage... preparing a noose.
*Has the hurt taken a toll on him, too, and by
death he's being seduced?*


Tried to open the doors, but they are locked.
Ran away again to find help, after I knocked.
Finally ran into Mr. Charles, who's always ready
to talk with his tongue cocked.
I'm sweaty and out of breath— with intensity
I'm stocked.

I'm trying to figure, who do I aim for, and who ain't got a shot?

Should I take Mr. Charles to Tim first, 'cause this is a lot!

Won't it be too late, what if he's hanging from that spot?

Or do I take him to the gym, 'cause there's a stabbing to block?

Should we split up— he take Sam, I take Pete — or is it better to swap?

Nah, that won't work, I need help, too; I'm a kid, not a cop.

I figured I'd take him to Sam, who's trying to kill a whole flock.

Before he began rambling, I yelled "Stop!"

I said, "You know Sam, the kid with the giant head and nose dripping with snot?

He has a suspicious box in his hand, make sure it doesn't drop!"

Then he said, "If we have to— grab his legs, and I'll grab him on top."

He tightened his belt, and had one pant leg in his sock.

Told Mr. Charles, "We need to hurry, we're on the clock."

We tried to get there as fast as we could, but he had that short leg hop.

265

He got tired in less than a minute, and walked the rest with that old man bop.

Took his hat off; guess it only takes thirty seconds for his dreads to become steaming hot.

Checked the bathroom, hoping Sam was still there, but he was not.

That's when another siren came on, and an announcement from the principal.

He said, "Now we're in a Shelter In," and to follow the steps that are permissible.

Not sure what permissible means, but a "Shelter In" is situational.

It could just be a safety precaution, or be because of something more criminal.

Mr. Charles said, "Let's get you back to class, you shouldn't be visible...

You got me checking bathrooms running around here in a circle, like it's critical."

I said, "I don't know why Sam isn't in the bathroom, it's inexplicable."

But told him to make sure to check the gym and auditorium; it was integral,

Because Pete and Tim are also on the verge of doing the unpredictable.

Hoping maybe all three were stopped would be a miracle.

266

Passed the water fountain, bent down for a sip — but it wasn't drinkable.

Mr. Charles' walkie talkie requested him to the rooftop, and I thought of the unthinkable.

He told me to continue to class, but my instinct to investigate was irresistible.

Should I leave this up to the adults? Not sure if I'm willing;

So as soon as Mr. Charles is gone, my direction I'm shifting.

Got me wondering— was there some blood spilling?

I couldn't handle the guilt if there was any killing.

I should've told Vanswoon from the beginning.

How in the world can an 11-year-old deal with this? Gotta be kidding.

I need to hurry to the third floor bathroom, before locks start clicking.

The third floor bathroom is close to the rooftop, you can hear and see everything.

I have to at least see that they're ok, since I couldn't stop things from occurring.

In my mind, I'm envisioning a body dangling from a rope turning and twisting,

Or some elaborate timing mechanism on a
bomb ticking.
Struggled up on the bathroom window ledge,
my weight I was lifting...
Opened the window, for a better angle, my
head I was tilting.

Thought I'd see a hand holding a box cutter
wielding.
Hold on... wait— there's a familiar voice I'm
hearing—
It wasn't Tim, Pete or Sam! It's Hank...
but what's he doing on top of the building???

# THE ROOFTOP

## Chapter 17

Hank sat on the edge with his feet dangling.
He can fall any moment, nothing to hold onto
for anchoring.
You can tell on his face, tears and sorrow
were hammering.
It was obvious, much pain he was managing.
I hear him complaining about this pain, saying,
"Even my name they're slandering."

Any toughness he had is completely
unraveling.
He fiddled with his fingers and clothes, not
sure he knows what's happening.
Then he looks at the sky, as if heaven he's
imagining.
Kept putting his head down, many thoughts he
must be examining.
He took it so hard, even with his life he's
gambling.
It appears that the hope of feeling better
he's abandoning.

It doesn't appear that his role in everything
that happened he's factoring.
I remember the things he did on the bus,
and it's baffling.
Because I know how he's feeling, in empathy
I'm inhabiting.
Looks like he's gotten bigger; I guess
depression is fattening.
I wish we would've known this kind of hurt
Hank is not fit to be handling.
All we cared about was to seeing their pride
and egos dismantling.
I can hear voices and feet in the background,
shuffling and scrambling.
Don't know why they sent Mr. Charles to the
rooftop, no time for rambling.
And I can smell Hank from the window; once
again, his inner skunk he's channeling.
Hurst, Doser, and Mr. Charles all are there,
but stayed back to keep things from
becoming more challenging.
Hank was banging his fist on his phone;  the
glass he's battering.
He requested no adults or cops, or on the
sidewalk he's splattering—
And they'll have to deal with his body parts
scattering.

270

Said he's only willing to talk to Mitch, or he's
not answering.
Hurst said Mitch is a child, and his life is not
worth shattering;
Then Hank made a gesture as if he was
slipping, or his legs were tangling.
He suddenly started slapping his own self, and
his neck he began strangling.
It appeared to be a threat, but there's no
time for haggling.
Should Hurst risk one life to save another?
This the decision he's tackling.
What if he loses both students? Such a loss
would be staggering.
To save both, would it cost his own life?
*Maybe*— these thoughts his conscious is
battling.
He pauses and rubs his head; his composure
he appears to be gathering.
All the stress must be the cause of the sweat
stains on his suit that are unflattering.

Then Hurst said ok, he'll get Mitch; his tone
was soothing and pampering,
He continued, "But we'll keep him at a
distance, or your request I'm canceling."

271

Mitch finally came, ushered up with Hurst's hands on his back.

Not surprised to see Mitch up there, with all the drama he attracts.

Hurst was in his ear the whole time, as if he was getting him ready for combat.

Seemed like the conversation was mostly "don't do this, don't do that!"

Mitch looked confused, and stared at Hank, who on the edge he sat;

Walking cautiously towards him, as if not wanting to slip on a mat—

Since the roof was on a down slope, slick and real flat.

He kept going, trying to remember what to say and where he was at.

For the most part, Mitch is a bearer of no tact.

In this terrifying situation, I'm wondering, *can he adapt?*


Mitch hesitated as if debating, should he be the one to distract?

Hank turned and gave Mitch a Medusa-like stare— enough to make a stone crack.

Hank seems to be anticipating an attack,

Because his fists were balled and his teeth clenched, ready for impact.

272

He looks uncomfortable and confused on how to act.

It's like he's looking at a puzzle, or a painting that's abstract.

He took a couple of small steps, as if it's a snake he must extract.

Mitch stopped within eight feet and softly stated, "Hurst said this is the closest we can interact."

By forcing those first words out, it probably helped some of his discomfort subtract.

Mitch said, "Why am I up here, Hank? Heard you wanted to chat…"

No response— Hank kept the silence and awkward intensity intact.

Mitch's voice was different, as if there was something he lacked.

Mitch continued, "Why are you up here? Why you tripping? And please be exact."

And Mitch waited for the details, opinions, or any other facts.


Full of sadness, you can tell Hank's patience is tapped;

And I think those were the wrong questions— 'cause right after that, Hank snapped.

He belted out, "YOU'RE THE REASON I'M UP HERE... YOU AND YOUR NERD PACK!!!.
The pain is intolerable, wish I can fall back;
I'm constantly agitated, annoyed, and can't seem to relax.
Damn— my fanny pack is empty— I should've refilled it with snacks!
It's hopeless; sometimes I feel like I'm trapped.
Death gotta be better than this; even thought of lying on the train tracks.

It might be just what I need to save me from this world;
No one will care if I'm dead, no emotions will be stirred.

Wish I was never born, and that my mom and pops never met.
Too bad there's no pause button on my life, or a way to press reset.

I want to get out of my house— this school—
I want to just press eject.
I wish I never had friends, I'm tired of living with regret.

One minute we're cool, then I'm the one you reject.
And speaking of snacks, I haven't even eaten yet.
I've been here for so long, I could eat a stray cat from the vet.
But eating doesn't soothe me anymore, it doesn't help me forget.
And I eat even more now, since I'm always upset.
Those posters, pics, songs and dances about me all over the internet…
I tried to tear them all down, and delete all the messages I would get.

I can't sleep; I keep envisioning the memes, so in midday I doze.
In class and in the caf, they shoot free throws when my crack's exposed.
Don't want to leave my room; you even made fun of my clothes.
Even on the bathroom stall walls, I see the riddle Myrtle composed."

Then all of a sudden, Hank began clawing at his own skin…

His scream must have released whatever's lurking within.
He charged toward Mitch, not sure what came over him;
I watched as he plowed through him; no clue what's about to begin.

Grabbing Mitch's collar, "I'm not meant for this world, I hurt so bad inside;
I want it to go away... I want to go to sleep for a very long time," he cried.
"I'm not afraid of death, I'm afraid of tomorrow.
I'm a coward, I should have done this a long time ago, and drowned out all of my sorrow...

Something keeps following me— keeps haunting me— it's misery.
I'm tired of trying, hope Mom and Dad can forgive me.

It consoles me to think of death; let's me know there is an end to the pain.
The memories torments my soul, it's like they're on repeat in my brain.

And I've felt death in everything, but death.

I anticipate rejection when I speak and I die, with every breath.

I listen to others' words, and their venom stings like never before.
When I eat, every bite is poisonous and seeping through every pore.
I cry and embrace death, because the pain I can no longer ignore.
When I sleep, I lie with death and nightmares always knocking on the door.
I experience death at home and at school, then shake death's hand on the way back from the store.
So, I'd rather not speak... listen... or breathe any more."

It's cold outside, but Hank is dripping with sweat.
Hank seems to be losing control; someone please cast a net.
He grabs Mitch's collar again; he's going to choke him, I bet.
He's filled with anger and sadness; his face was red like the tip of a cigarette.
He grunts the words, "Help me or else..."
Mitch grunts back, "Is that a threat?"

Hanks screams, "You owe me— you used to be my friend— now pay your debt!"

Mitch began to bark, "What do you want from me... what do you want me to say?"
Then grabbed Hank's hands from his collar and ripped them away.
"What you wanna hear? I'm sorry? But when you did it, it was okay?
How is it our fault for the ton that you weigh?
Nobody made you go for seconds at the All-You-Can-Eat Buffet!
No one told you not to bathe, or not use a deodorant stick or spray!"
Hank interrupted, grabbed Mitch saying, "You want me to do it, then let me get it underway!"
And looked lost like his thoughts were in complete disarray.
He continued, "You think I'm a punk!"
Mitch growled, "Get off me, I think you should go pray!"
Hank grunted back, "They wanna see me do it, too... where are they?
You must want me to jump, be buried underground with worms to rot and decay...

Without any flowers, without a single bouquet!

You wanna see me turn into ash, like you find in an ashtray.

You'd love to find me dead, and dumped in the trunk of a Chevrolet!"

Mitch disputed with, "Nah, my dude. Yo, you cray-cray!

We both made fun of people, and put our hands on them everyday!

And when it's done to you— you can't handle what's in play!

Imagine how they must have felt with us in the way,

But they ain't try to jump off a roof when their clouds were grey—

Or suffocate themselves and make their breathing delayed."

Mockingly, Mitch continues, "Now you want to turn around and claim that I've betrayed!"

With a finger on Hanks chest, "We just got tired of being the victims,

so we decided to repay!

I used to be one of those kids on who bullies would prey!

Because of it, I hated grammar school, and decided to disobey!

You gotta man up, you ain't the only one who had it rough at home, or wherever you stay.
While I was sleeping, my dad used to rip the covers off and beat me where I lay.

Sometimes I worry he won't come home;
Scared he'd leave like my Mama did, so I weep till my pillow's soaked.
But then Pops up the next day smelling like booze and smoke.
You think your life is a joke!
Please! Some mornings I'm starving, no food to eat and our EBT card gets revoked.
Tried to steal money from his wallet for lunch a few times, but he's always broke."
They are still grilling each other; violent responses they begin to provoke.
All this screaming back and forth got these pigeons afloat!
For a brief moment, all you heard were some faint voices and the flag, waving like a cloak.
Now sirens are blaring; I'm glad Hurst didn't hear the words Mitch spoke.
Mr. Charles is over there shaking from the cold, like he was having a stroke.

By now, there are people watching; a couple
of kids, and a few grown folk.
And you can see some faces watching from
their windows, while a few heads poke.
An ambulance, a fire truck, and the cops just
pulled up— just in case it's not a hoax.

Mitch disputed, "See, I can relate, but
suicide ain't the answer.
There are people with worse problems, some
people fighting through cancer.
There are things wrong with me too, that I
would love to transfer.
For example, my eyes are so spread apart, I
can have one on New York and one on New
Hampshire!
I'm a four-foot midget, and a horrible dancer!

What you're doing don't make any sense, stop
acting like a rook!
You should just tear out a page— don't throw
out the whole book!

You might be in foul trouble, but you don't
quit the whole game.
If the pilot is sick, they don't crash the whole
plane.

Even after a whole losing season, you don't get rid of the whole team, fire the coach.
Just like you don't throw out a whole box of cereal over one little roach.

Don't throw out a bag of candy because a couple got smushed.
You better not had called me up here so you can get pushed.

You wouldn't be ending the pain, you'd pass it on to your friends and family; they wouldn't be off the hook.
And they would feel responsible just 'cause you got shook.
You'll leave them consumed with shame and guilt; that wouldn't be a good look.
They won't remember how you lived, but only how you 'got took'.
Death will steal your chance to make things better, like a straight up crook."

With tears in his eyes, Hank rambled, "But what I want does not exist.
What school can I go to and avoid the detention or suspension list?

How can I see or smell food and find a way to resist?

There's no girl coming up to me wanting to get kissed…

There's no place I can go and never get dissed…

There's no home I can go to and never get pissed…

No friends I can chill with, and not be dismissed."

Mitch said, "That's 'cause you're looking in the wrong places…you need an assist."


Then Mitch paused, as if he remembered Hurst's words and its scope.

He said, "I don't wanna argue any more, how about you?" Hank said, "Nope!"

Put his arms around him and said, "We're good, don't sit up here being a mope."

Mitch joked and said, "Let's get off this roof and I'll buy you a bar of soap."

Then I saw the first sign that Hank could finally cope.

And they gave each other a hug and I thought that was dope!

Then all of a sudden… Mitch slipped… slid down the flat slope!

Hank was shocked, hands on his face as his
cheeks flushed to the color of taupe.
A lady who saw it screamed and started
praying maybe to Jesus, Allah or perhaps the
Pope.
Mitch hung from the edge of the roof,
dangling like rope,
Scratching the cement, but with his left hand,
a strip of metal ledge he groped...
Yelling for help, and clinging on to slim hope.

# Resolved Anxiety

## Chapter 18

The lock down drill is over so I left the third floor bathroom as quickly as I could.
Snuck passed a janitor, who by the stairs stood;
Told him I was stuck in the bathroom, like a broken elevator in the hood.
Thought to check the first floor bathroom for Sam again, but nah, I'm good.

Opened the classroom door, with a guerrilla soldier-like intro.
Everything that just happened still got my thoughts in limbo.
Vanswoon is keeping the kids from looking outside the window.
Before I could sit down, I was being bombarded for some info.

Like, "Why is there an ambulance outside?"
"Did somebody get hurt?" and, Who died?

And how about, "Is everyone ok?..."
"Obviously not," I replied.
Can't take all these questions, so, I did what
most of you would do— I lied.
Said I was locked in the third floor
bathroom, as if bail was denied.
It wouldn't open, no matter how hard I tried.
With that aside...
Look who's sitting there like Dr. Jekyll trying
to contain Hyde!
With another pair of sneakers on the side,
the laces ripped and untied;
It's Mr. Box Cutter! I wonder if the stabbing
was denied?
Maybe he washed the blood off and his hands
and clothes dried;
His head stayed straight forward, as if a
ghost he eyed...
Or, maybe stuck in a trance as if he saw his
future bride.
His face is reddish-pink looking deep-fried.
In my direction, Vanswoon through her
glasses spied.
She must know I have something to tell her;
it's overwhelming like a tide.
*Once I say something, who'll protect me when
my face and his fist collide?*

*What if the damage is already done? It certainly won't put back tears that cried.*

She slithered over with that evil scowl and glide.

Whatever I'm going to say, I have about eight seconds to decide;

It's down to seven seconds, I looked around for a place to hide...

Six seconds— should I run or sink into a seat slide?

Five seconds— for withholding information saw myself in the back of a cop car taking a ride.

Four seconds— I can feel beads of sweat from my backside divide.

Three seconds— took two deep breaths that sounded as if I sighed.

Two seconds— trying to grab hold of my last bit of pride...

One second— my heart is on the edge, jumping from the place it resides...

Before she said a word, I muttered, "Can I speak to you in private?"
I'm about to dive right in like a kamikaze pilot.

Feel like a big girl with her favorite meal before she goes on a diet,
Or like I'm skydiving in a hurricane type of climate.
I noted, "I have something to tell you, but I'm not trying to start a riot.
Someone in the class has a weapon on them," and I gestured slow and quiet.

She called Pete to the door, who seemed startled at first.
Now he's looking pissed, and must have mumbled a curse.
Face always red from all those pimples that burst;
Vanswoon checked his pockets and bag, like she was checking her own purse.
At this point, he's even more annoyed and almost did a reverse.
He told her about the box cutter, after being coerced.
He said someone tied his sneakers to the basketball hoop,
And that he needed the box cutter to cut each loop.

I responded with, "What?" and was about to interrupt,

288

Then remembered he had a pair of sneakers by his desk with the laces cut.

The bell rang, and it was announced there will be an early dismissal.
Upon hearing this, everyone shot out the classroom like missiles.

As I entered the hallway, I notice one class was still in session.
It was the science class, and it wasn't a regular lesson.
Why was Sam in front of the class is my first question.
And on his face, why is there such a nervous expression?
As if he's in front of the whole congregation for confession.
*Is this the part he blows everyone up in this section?*
Why is this other kid mocking Sam sitting in his direction,
And another looking at me, as if he's on the verge of defection?
Between the teacher's clipboard and words on the board, is there a connection?

I'm guessing students were still giving
presentations, and awaiting corrections.

And the last one to go is Sam, I suspect.
He has that weird contraption with him—
what the heck?
I flashback to Sam in the bathroom with
that mysterious object.
I see now, it's not a bomb he had; it was his
science project.

On the way toward the exit, I will pass the
auditorium doors.
*Should I check to see if there's a body dangling
over the stage floor?*

I can see the auditorium doors about 50 feet
away.
The closer I get, feels like I'm walking in a
cemetery instead of a hallway;
Like I'm walking in water, or through quick
sand is the way—
Or perhaps shuffling through a mud pit, or
feet sinking in wet clay.

Now I'm within 25 feet, and I'm dying to turn
back;
Looked around for a short cut, or detour,
where I'd end up on the track.
It's like I'm walking toward the beanstalk and
my first name is Jack;
Or approaching the beachhead right before
an invasion or attack.

Within 10 feet now, and I'm trying to convince
myself to see it through.
The pep talk sounded more like, "You know
how you do?
You got this, it will all be over in a few.
One quick look, then keep it moving— boy,
that's all you."

I opened the door, saw Tim and a few others
fussing with a net.
There was one black girl, two Spanish kids
and one brunette.
The black girl is telling the others what to
get.

*What am I missing here, did they thwart off the threat?*

The noose was there, but it wasn't around Tim's neck.

The chair he stood on was gone— hold up... wait a sec...

They were prepping the stage for the school play, how could I forget?

He wasn't trying to hang himself, he was creating props for the set!

I reached the exit doors, and the ambulance was still there.

There were also a couple of news cameras, and I avoided the pair;

About half a dozen police officers with Hurst, and confusion in the air.

Some onlookers, nosy neighbors and pigeons scattered everywhere.

Later that evening, after dinner, Pops and I were watching SmackDown.

When it was over, the news came on, and at the same time Mama came around.

Pops was knocked out sleeping on the couch, looking real uncomfortable— neck all bent— ouch!
No! It can't be, please I hope I heard wrong!
Guess what the lead on the news is, as Mama is passing along?...

What happened at our school today and now I'm focused...
On finding the remote, or changing the channel before she'd notice.

Did it fall between the couch? Maybe Pops left it in the bathroom.
Doesn't Mama need to ask me what happened, or would she assume?
Oh no, she's watching, and they're interviewing witnesses.
She says a couple of "uh ohs" and "oh my goodnesses."

Here it is, found it... the whole time it was underneath the chair.
But before I could change the channel, Mama goes— "Don't you dare!"
Then watches the rest in disbelief, and in full stare,

293

While I'm sitting there hoping we have a blackout, but that's pretty rare.

She asks, "Did you know about any of this? Is that why you were early dismissed?"

Do I tell her the truth? It got so quiet, I could hear myself swallow.
If I tell her a half-truth, more questions will follow.
If I lie and say I know nothing, she'll see right through me like I'm hollow.
"Isn't that Mitch kid your friend?" she continued with sorrow.

The last question she asked, as if she needed more proof,
"Did you know the principal saved him from falling off the roof?"

# Bully Remorse

## Chapter 19

It's a brand new week, and there's a few
things I'm discovering.
I'm feeling worse and worse, seeing the
bullies still suffering;

I'd rather catch the flu and be in bed for a
week,
Or, be exposed and everyone sees my
underwear's doodoo streak.

No, I'm lying! I couldn't handle that either!
It's almost like I got a girdle on, because I
need a breather.

I looked at Carl during class, he is fidgeting
and flustering;
He spoke to himself, I had no idea what he
was muttering.

Sounding like voices from the mind of a
schizophrenic.
His tapping is sounding like a morse code
that's real authentic.

I said, "What's wrong?" Then he gave a long
sigh and began stuttering,
While his feet under his seat are scuffling.
He looked up at the ceiling as if a UFO is
hovering
And said, "I-I-I-I'm not s-s-sure, but it's
smothering.

If my dad finds out, what will happen to me?
Who knows.
He might make me spend another year
wearing theses dorky old clothes.
He might never let me get surgery on my
sausage like nose,
And not knowing when, for me feels like the
end— guess that's the way it goes."
I said, "At worst, we'll get suspended," then
he put his head down and shut his eyes
closed.

Then Myrtle and Suzie came up to me,
"What's up with you and Carl, mister?"

Myrtle is staring at me like she wants me to kiss her;
But that ain't happening, I'd rather kiss my own sister.
She said, "You two are in the middle of class engaged in a less-than-ambiguous whisper."

I didn't know what ambiguous meant, but I nodded
while staring at Suzie's chin whisker
That looked like a feather for a tickler.
I said, "Carl has a problem with what we did," and Suzie affirmed, "Yeah we figured.
Myrtle and I spoke, and we're no longer happy with the message that's being delivered...
Seeing the result of what we've done makes me uncomfortable like a blister.
Not sure if it's stress or gas, but I'm getting a burning sensation in my liver.
Matter of fact, every time I think about it, I start to feel sicker.
The thought of losing any school time, makes my hand tremble and spine quiver...
And if this affects my grades or honor roll, I'll be more than bitter.
If this leads to suspension, I'll beg them to reconsider.

Lately I've had a hard time looking in the
mirror,
Part of me is proud of what I did, the other
part of me begs to differ.
Never got in any trouble before; I'm the girl
with the 'great job' sticker.
The girl with the eyeglass glitter,
First on the debate team, and spelling bee
winner.
What would my parents think? This type of
news is a killer."
Then she stormed off— something must have
hit a trigger.

In the hallway I bumped into Stick.
Always wearing a jersey, this time of a New
York Knick.
He walked alongside me and spoke low, yet
quick.
As if he had to tell me I had a booger to pick,
Or as if he's trying to set someone up with a
trick.
He asked me, how was I doing, and how was
the whole clique?
He expressed that he's now troubled by the
pain that we did indeed, inflict.

"It's not fun anymore; I get upset when I receive a text, meme or pic.
It's a feeling that hits the chest like a kangaroo kick,
And sits heavy in my stomach, like I swallowed a brick.

I can't be seen with you, they'll be onto us; let's pick our spots.
You weren't in class; Hank and Mitch were on the news, they'll connect the dots."
Then he took his fists and against the locker, he took shots.

After school Flakes came and sat next to me on the bus.
He had a different look on his face, like he had something to discuss.
Said he doesn't feel like dancing, everything is different; he needs time to adjust.
At first, I thought he was referring to his shampoo that's not helping his scalp crust.
Instead he said, "Hank is not here, and it's all because of us."
He seemed a little angry, and this was the first time I heard him cuss.

He said, "What we did took guts, but ruining
lives wasn't the purpose.
Everything we did, now I see can be
dangerous,
and I'm a little nervous."

He looked away and from the corner of his
eye, I saw a tear.
Then he got up and sat in another seat,
further back toward the rear.

Later that night, I called Mitch on the phone.
I told him how the others felt, and their need
to atone.

Spoke about the guilt they're dealing with,
how it caught them by surprise;
Awaiting further consequences has them
anticipating their demise.

It's like in the old days, waiting to get stoned;
Or after you eat those murder burgers and
you're waiting to hit the throne.
"If Mama finds out, for sure I will be
disowned.
She'll probably beat me while saying, 'You
think you're grown!'"

Mitch responded with, "Yeah, I know what they're feeling like;
It's like I'm a batter and I'm sitting on two strikes...

Being on that roof with Hank helped me realize a lot;
Namely, that revenge only added dangerous curves to the plot.

It's been a long week; not something I want to talk about.
Maybe some other time; sorry Homie— I'm out."

"Mitch you still there?" The way he hung up was so abrupt.
Was it something I said, did I make a mistake or did I interrupt?
I kept calling him back, but no one would pick up.

# THE SOLUTION

## Chapter 20

The next day is a Friday; the weekend was
almost here.
Seems like we avoided a catastrophe, though
I'm still sensing some fear.
It didn't feel like a regular Friday; it felt like
judgment day of the worst year.
It felt like a day that would bring on
something more severe,
Or a day to walk on pins and needles, for what?
— It's unclear.
Afraid the weekend will be ruined, or
something will appear.

And what do you know, before the bell blasts,
Even before the teacher gives us our task,

The class phone rang; Vanswoon said Hurst
wants to see me in his office.
He also sent for Mitch, Myrtle, Suzie, Stick
and Carl, and look who came for us....

Mr. Charles pops up to bring us down, and now I'm feeling nauseous.
I can feel the fear seeping through my skin like it's porous.

They couldn't find Flakes, who's always dancing in the hallway using the bathroom pass.
Matt was with the nurse, because he's allergic to grass.
The school lawn was cut this morning and Matt looked like he needed a mask.
Why are we being escorted to the office?— No one bothered to ask.

We walked in one at a time, as if getting ready for a police lineup.
Each one of us hesitating through the doorway; for this we didn't sign up.

It was as if we're walking to the guillotine, scared and reluctant;
Or spent years sinning, and now we're at the gates of heaven waiting for judgment.

Mr. Charles had to give a couple of us a nudging;
While shaking his head full of dreads, in his

old school ways he's judging.

We all sat in Hurst's office; he wasn't even in
there, yet.
As I looked around the room, I felt some
sense of regret;
But I also got the sense we all knew what to
expect.
He had one too many ashtrays, his last name
might as well be "Cigarette".

He had a whole bunch of chairs in there, as if
he was expecting a large group.
Maybe a small orchestra, a sports team, or a
bunch of Girl Scout troops.

Perhaps expecting a bunch of kids, that've
been up to no good.
Flakes finally came, and for the first time,
without dancing he stood.
Matt wheeled his chair in, he was so nervous,
he kept knocking into the wood.

Like an old guard dog, Mr. Charles kept an eye
on everybody.
It was real quiet, like when a bunch of boys
spot a real hottie.

304

Anxiety is building, and to everyone's nervous habits, I take heed.
Flakes is biting his nails and spitting them out like sunflower seeds...

Suzie is twirling her hair....
Myrtle is rocking back and forth, like she's in a rocking chair...

Mitch is tapping his fingers sounding like roaches tap dancing...
Carl is grinding his teeth, and it sounded like rocks making out or against the concrete advancing.

Stick has no lips, but he keeps biting them, and it looks like he's biting his own chin.
Matt is chewing on pen tops, as if they were barbecue chicken.

Butterflies stop, dropped and rolled in my stomach, as if there's a fire in there.
So much so, it could've been me when a strange smell began creeping through the air.
Did someone fart in this tiny room, with the windows closed? That ain't fair.

It was like there was a stinky ghost
circulating the room—
Or someone stepped in dog crap— or had on
butt-crack scented perfume.
Did a sewer explode, but no one heard a boom?
It smelled like feces cooking on the hot
concrete in the middle of June.

Finally Hurst walks in, and he made a face like
he smelled it, too.
I can tell he was more upset than usual; God
knows what he's about to do.

Carl began crying, even before the first
question was asked.
As I'm staring at Hurst's mustache,
I noticed when he speaks it wiggles and flaps.
There's a fly over our heads doing laps,
Zig-zagging through Mr. Charles' dreads as it
passed.
Hurst said, "We've investigated a situation
where four students were being harassed,
With pictures, dances and songs, and internet
hacks...
Name-calling, intimidation, isolation, all types
of attacks."

Suzie interrupted with, "Before you go on, you
should stop.
Before you accuse me of anything, let me
remind you my daddy's a cop."

Hurst ignored it, "I can't believe some of my
best students committed these acts.
My honor students, kids on the Principal's List...
these can't be facts?"

Myrtle tried to interrupt, trying to plead her
case—
With— "Hold up, sir, some of this is off base.
We were simply defending ourselves in the
first place."

Hurst continued, "I've called every last one of
your guardians, moms and paps.
You guys must've had the biggest brain fart, or
the longest mental lapse.
Every time I think of suspending all eight of
you, it feels like I'm gonna collapse."
Not sure if it was anger or disappointment, but
all of a sudden, the desk he slaps.

After that, Carl's crying got worse;

He put on a crying clinic, and none of it was rehearsed.
He started with the lip trembling cry, like his bottom lip was having a seizure.
Then goes into the whining cry, that sounds like a toddler pleading to his teacher.

Hurst insisted, "Before I go any further, let's hear your side of the story— you have the floor."
I decided to speak before Suzie made his eardrums sore.
Told Hurst, "They bullied us first, did things we couldn't ignore.
They locked Stanley in a locker, gave Matt two wheelchair tire flats, and wait there's more...
There were signs on Stanley's back, ink in Myrtle's teeth, and fake bugs swimming in Suzie's tray, short of needing an oar.
No one came to our defense, and we were afraid to tell a teacher— therefore;
Mitch and I decided to form a team of everyone they bullied from before,
And take revenge on these bullies— fight back— we felt this was war!

Do to them, what they did to us, but even more hardcore.
What we didn't expect was the effect on their self-esteem that we tore."
We told Hurst we were sorry, and it wouldn't happen again— we swore.
Hurst's jaw clinched up, as if trying to contain a hungry lioness' roar;
Then he got up and paced around the room, while mysteriously staring at the door.

At this point,  Carl is on his snot bubbling cry;
as if he's chewing gum, blowing bubbles out his nostril.
Now he's quiet; his mouth is wide open, then a sudden burst of cry has us all startled.

Hurst asserted, "I understand you all felt what you did was right.
I like how each one of you found your own way to fight,
And how you guys found a common cause for ya'll to unite.
But, you were foolish for being bullish and that's me being polite."

There goes that fly again, bugging us like we're fruit at the supermarket.

Trying to land on Hurst's mustache, it must think it's a magic carpet.

Hurst turned to Myrtle, "You'll always be the ones who end up being punished, despite—
The fact they did it first, doesn't excuse this oversight.
You can't do what they did, because it might cause tensions to flare and emotions ignite."

Now Carl is on his "I can't breathe cry"; this boy has asthma, he better not die.
*He has the hiccups now?* No, he's on to the hiccups cry;
Then goes into the exaggerated cry, sounding like he lost everything, no lie.

Then more words of advice came from the mouth of Hurst.
He spoke like he wrote a book and was spitting out a verse.
"Yes, we all have different issues; that's what makes us diverse.
You need to get to know one another, and try to converse.

Find things you have in common; we're all the same, just different colors.
See what your prejudices are, and how it affects others...

Try to understand what others feel like, and respect their views.
Realize what would you feel like, put yourself in their shoes.
Show compassion, be kind— with that, you'll never lose."

First parents to show up had to be mine.
*Dear Lord, if I'm going to die today, please send me a sign.*

Mama came with the drama, and her two belt straps;
And Pops still had drool on his chin from his afternoon naps.

Mama is prepping herself for her parent— teacher conference skit.
Acting like she doesn't speak English, and only says "ok" and "thank you," but that's it.

Hurst disclosed, "And as far 'snitching' is concerned, let me make this plain...

Criminals use this word to commit crimes
and keep witnesses under restrain.
Snitching and getting help just ain't the
same, let me explain."

*What was that?* Skirted on the floor from
behind Mama's pocket book...
*Did it come from our house and in Mama's
purse a ride here it took?*
While Hurst is talking, for this daredevil
roach I look...

Hurst stood up, "Snitching came from the
mafia. It's telling on someone for personal
gain...
Getting help is to prevent someone from
dishing out pain...
To themselves, or to others, which is more
humane."

Carl's dad just walked in smelling like a
smoke stack;
Looking like an accountant had a baby with a
lumberjack.

He had the hairiest ears; on them looked
like thick moss,

And a couple of long ones that looked like strings of grey floss...
And his eyebrows were two squirrel tails and on his forehead they lie across...
With a Yakama sitting on the part of his head suffering from hair loss.

Hurst looked at Mitch, "If you're afraid of the wrath that comes from getting help and you want to stay in your lane...
There are ways you can do it anonymously, your safety we'll maintain.

We have an anonymous dropbox in the Main Office for bullying reports, if you need to complain.
And there are anonymous apps and hotlines, part of an anti-bullying campaign."

At this point, Myrtle's parents walked in, but didn't want to sit.
I couldn't understand when they spoke, because of their accent, I'll admit.
There goes that roach playing peekaboo, like it's too legit to quit!
Picked my book bag off the floor, so it doesn't go in it.

Hurst continued, "And if you still think getting help will make matters worse,
As long as you organize, and go as a group, no one has to be first.

They can't say you snitched if it's six of you, or whoever;
It's rather filing a complaint, or taking a stand together.
It's like sending a letter to the mayor, to do better.

The more, the merrier— you can apply even more pressure.
There is strength in numbers; the bullying will become lesser.
Whether you go to the assistant principal, the dean or your professor,
Make sure you have proof of the truth from your oppressor."

As soon as Mitch's dad shows up, on his breath you can smell the vodka.
He didn't even know where Mitch was, so Mitch had to say, "Poppa!"

His clothes are all dirty; I think he told me his

pops is a mechanic.

He must have swallowed a full grown midget, his stomach was gigantic!

He had the biggest tooth gap, it was like a canal for the Titanic.

He smelled like he was swimming in an ocean of gasoline, as big as the Atlantic.

Now I look at Mitch, and he seems like he's about to panic…

And that fly must've found a new friend, because around Mitch's dad it flew.

It kept bouncing off his face, like it was love at first sight between the two.

Hurst to clarify said, "Just in case you don't know what bullying is…

Let me break it down like I'm preparing you for a quiz—

Name-calling and teasing is bullying, this is true.

Physical intimidation is bullying, if you do that, you're through."

*Who's this?* "I'm Fernando's aunt," is how she introduces herself.

She walks in, dressed real strange, like a gypsy or a Puerto Rican elf.

315

Hurst shook her hand, and commenced back to the chew.
Said, "Yeah, it's bullying, everything you drew.
Even the butt-crack free throws people threw.
It's bullying— posting embarrassing things on social media for everyone to view.
Even isolation from the majority, and excluding a few;
Even forming a gang, or becoming a crew is bullying, too.
So is writing songs about people, and referring to names we knew.
Oh, and can't forget those embarrassing pranks you do!
Even creating ridiculous dances, and— yup, mocking too."

Matt's parents came in looking ridiculous, with matching shirts and slacks.
Looking like an unemployed figure skating team, and those are facts.

Or, a broke country music duo...
Better yet— a pair of playing cards— you know, the ones that say UNO.

Hurst said, "See, bullying is an imbalance of power, that's the first clue.
If you want it to stop, here's what you must do.
There are four strategies that will empower you.
React opposite of what they want, if you want it to undo.

When you're insulted or made fun of, don't get mad, or insult them right back.
First strategy is to laugh hysterically when it happens, and walk away— they'll never expect that!"

*Hmmm… is that what the Weiner kid was doing?*
He only laughed when the joke was on him, and kept it moving.
They thought he was a loser, and found him amusing.
But they only got one joke in, so who was really losing?
There goes my friend again, now Flakes sees it, too.
Our roach friend was moonwalking right by Flakes' shoe.

Hurst said, "You can also give them a blank, emotionless stare and walk away.
Because if you act like it bothers you, then the bullies will stay.

Mitch goes, "Yeah, like Weird Wendy does—
you mean this whole time she was fooling?
She reacts like a zombie and I swear it's confusing!
We couldn't tell if she was about to snap, or if she'd been using.
It wasn't fun clowning her, our good times she was ruining."

Hurst continued, "The third strategy is a preemptive strike.
 Before they insult you, crack jokes on your own self, as if it's Open Mic."

Stick acknowledged, "Oh, I think I saw that in a movie flick!
Say it before they say it, and they'll have nothing to say slick.
Take their ammo away, and you'll shut them up quick.
And swiftly walk away— yeah, that's one hell of a trick!"

And there goes that fly buzzing around Suzie's ear…
She shooed it off like it was a no-carb diet that was near.
At this point, everyone is annoyed hoping it disappears.

Hurst concluded, "The last strategy might be the most effective.
Compliment them, be nice; at first they may not seem receptive.

But no one can keep being mean to someone who's nice to them;
You will at the very least, bring the bullying down to a five, from a ten."
Myrtle said, "I don't know about this one, not everyone can be Sarah-Sweet."
How do you compliment someone who's attacking you, whenever you meet?

 How can we not get upset?
And how can we forget?"

An old lady walks in and says, "I'm here for my grandson, Stanley."
Mr. Charles helps her to a seat, while she chews on her gums like candy.
319

She was making weird sounds, not sure if it
was sinuses, or if she was clearing her throat.
She's wearing a jacket that must be made
from the hairs of goat.

Hurst's phone is ringing— not a bad time for
a phone call.
That roach is about to skydive into Stanley's
grandmother's wig from off the wall!

Hurst refuted, "They are not attacking you,
they're attacking what you represent.
They're unhappy with themselves, they're
filled with discontent.
You represent an opportunity for them to
feel better about themselves, 100%.
It makes them feel powerful, because they're
controlling your feelings through torment.
So, control is the intent...
Don't take it personally, they don't know the
real you; so for you it wasn't meant.
Sometimes they're just doing what was done
to them, that they couldn't prevent.
Bullies have been hurt, insulted, neglected,
violated to an extent.

So don't get mad, it's them you should
actually feel bad for.
Remember that, and don't react to it
anymore."


Hurst's office felt like a funeral home
surrounded by caskets, or a room filled with
traps;
Made for scared children, not for the usual
rats.
Tension stood at attention in the middle of
the room, with fear breathing down our
backs.
Even the sounds from Matt's wheelchair
sound scary when it creeks and cracks.


There's a picture on Hurst's desk, I'm not
sure if it's his son or daughter.
I've been wondering for a while now, it's like
deciding if it's sprite or water.
I saw strong bone structure, and long hair; it
would be different if it was shorter.
Boy or girl, I'm not leaning toward either-or;
I'm on the border.


At the same time, I'm looking and wondering
what happened to that daredevil roach?

Was he stepped on? Is he on a first-class
flight to heaven? Really, more like coach...

Did he and that annoying fly link up, break
bread and now they're making a toast?
Or perhaps taking selfies together, hashtag—
bestfriendgoals for an Instagram post?...

What's taking him so long to decide our fate?
We've been in his office for over 30 minutes
and we still have to wait.
Anticipating these consequences feels like on
my chest there's a one-hundred pound weight.

In walks Suzie's dad, still in uniform— and
fresh from playing Cops and Robbers.
His front teeth looked like a row of white
MINI Coopers— he had the biggest choppers!

Oh my God! After all the advice Hurst just
said,
I assume it would have an impact on me, but
instead...
Every parent that's walked in, with my
thoughts I've shred.
I can't believe it! All this time I've been
BULLYING inside my head...

How Suzie's dad walked in was to intimidate,
based on everybody's reaction.
He asked to speak to the principal outside; you
can see on Suzie's face the satisfaction.

When Hurst came back in, he looked as if he
was ready for action.
If it was a picture, "The moment before our
lives ended," would be the caption.

Principal Hurst explained to the parents what
the E.C.A.B. Anti-Bullying Program was about.
Here it is, one after another, our punishments
are dished out.

Each parent staring down their child, the way a
boxer does right before a bout...
Penalty after penalty, and if we looked at the
score, it would be a complete rout.

He handed out suspensions, not one day, or two
days; but really, a whole week?
Someone burst out in a shout, It was Myrtle,
as if she was kicked in the oblique.
He started cutting out all clubs and activities.
He then cut out events and special assemblies.

Myrtle appealed, "I'm on the Debate Team."
He countered, "For two weeks that's cut."
"Not the school dance!" Myrtle pleaded so
abrupt...

He objected, "Yes, the school dance too, and
please don't interrupt.
Even the Chess Club," and then Carl looked
up.
"Don't even think about playing ball," Stanley
put his head down, "Yeah, that's shut.
You're off the school newspaper committee."
Then Matt said, "What?"
Myrtle sat there looking so distraught from
the result.
She closed her eyes to prevent a flow from
her tear duct.
Mr. Charles looks like insubordination he
wants to conduct.
Seeing how everyone, especially Myrtle's,
emotions were struck.

And just when I thought he was done
He said, "Everyone will have a week of
suspension, and a week of detention, so have
fun.

Because you know what you'll be doing." *Out this room, I'm ready to run…*

"You'll be writing apology letters to each and every single one.

But for you two, Mitch and Daniel, it still won't be over.
You will also have community service, since you two were the composers."

After one riddle was solved, towards us the picture he spun
And said, "I know how you parents feel— I go through the same with my own son."

As we all got up to leave, I'm still wondering where that daredevil roach was at.
There he goes— underneath Carl's dad's shoe! He lay flat.
And guess who was first out the door like a miniature bat?
He wasn't a fly after all— he is a muscle-bound gnat!

# UNEXPECTED SENSIBILITIES

## Chapter 21

After a week of suspension, we had another full week of detention.
The plan was to be separated, but this they forgot to mention.

Mitch and I will soon start our community service.
I'm volunteering at a Meal Center, and Mitch at a Nursing Home, and I'm nervous.
Since we are the ones that orchestrated the whole circus,
We ended up being bullies too, which wasn't the purpose.

Haven't seen or heard from anyone in two weeks.
My sister thought the whole thing was funny and mocks me every time she speaks.

Calling me "Trey Strong" and "Dumbo Slice";
"I wonder what is must be like to be Scrawny
Spice."

She called me "Bonny Mayweather" saying,
"Oh, now you think you're different?"
Any little thing that happens, she refers back
to the incident...

If I ask for some paper, she says, "Oh, now
you want to draw pics of me?"
If I put on music, "Oh, you looking for ideas
to write more songs about what you see?"

If I knock on the door while she's in the
bathroom, "Let me get out before I'm duct-
taped to the toilet."
If we're eating pancakes, "Let me pour the
syrup for you before people start talking
about how I wore it."

Back in the caf, it appears nothing is
different;
Some of the boys who were aggressive are
still belligerent.
Mitch was there, so were a few from his
former crew, but everyone is distant.

It seems like I'm not the only one alert, my observations are vigilant.
Today they were serving fake chicken patties and a pizza equivalent.
Some of the comments I'm hearing are still completely ignorant.
Flakes was moving slower, as if he sprained a ligament.
Some of the kids are still sectioned off, especially the immigrants.
Mr. Charles is still walking by, telling stories and being militant,
Pointing out everything in the school system that he sees as discriminant...
Like, only white people have red hair— that's why red ink is used for grading; it's a form of imprisonment.
Felt something in the air, as if another incident is imminent.
I evesdropped on a few conversations and their participants.

It appears some things happened while we were suspended;
There were some copycat situations, not sure if they were intended.

One conversation was about some kid, who I
assume, Vanswoon's class he attended—
Who got sent to Hurst's office for a pic that
made Vanswoon feel offended.
The pic was of Mrs. Vanswoon; he must not
have been afraid, or at least he pretended.
He had it circulating in the classroom, while to
the lesson she tended.
Another said, "You know, Vanswoon has eyes
like a hawk," but more like a vulture she
descended.
She has ears like a Rottweiler, she's why a
whisper was invented.
So she intercepted it, and the picture was
apprehended.

One girl said, "I heard Rachel created a
poster of some girl in her class."
Another one was like, "They took a picture and
posted it, and put her on blast."
Two more girls responded, "It wasn't just a
pic, it was a meme they realized, at last.
The girl's parents found out and filed a
complaint, for being harassed."

Someone else was like, "No it wasn't Rachel, it
was Kelly."

While listening, the story must have changed six times; it went from Rachel to Kelly-to Shelly.
Then Shelly turned into Sharon, and Sharon turned into Shereen;
And it went from a poster to a pic, now to a meme!

Hold on, is our little bully revolt the cause of this?
I hope we didn't give bullies more ideas to apply to their victim's list.
It's been two weeks— what we did, will it be used to assist?
Is it related? Maybe everyone forgot about our diss.
It could just be coincidence, but I guess it's hard to dismiss.
They're probably just making it up, to spread rumors they can't seem to resist.
I already said I'm sorry, but can regret and satisfaction inside me coexist?

I hope kids who stand up for themselves don't become bullies and prey on the weaker.
All of a sudden, an announcement was made on the loud speaker.

It was Hurst, but can hardly hear— the cafeteria noise is getting steeper.
Oh boy, he sounds upset, and the base in his voice is deeper.

Who did what now? We haven't even made it to spring.
The girls to my left won't stop talking, doing their Chatty Patty thing.

I tried to strain my ears to hear,
But only one thing was made clear;
I think he summoned every class to an emergency assembly, but to where I didn't hear.

Then for some reason on their faces, the cafeteria staff wore worry;
They seemed to be in a hurry, every action was a scurry.

They started closing off the kitchen, much sooner than usual.
They even moved a couple of tables around, as if to make it more suitable.
Maybe the period is ending early; for what?
Nah, that seems delusional.

Did Hurst call for everyone to meet in the
auditorium, maybe outside by the track?
Mr. Dozer's class is walking in; they already ate
lunch, guess they were told to come back.
And there's Vanswoon with her class, too, and
then the rest of the teachers; now it's packed.
This must be where Hurst wanted everyone to
meet at.

Hurst finally comes in and his face is
overwhelmed with emotion.
He grabs the microphone and stands on top of
a table to settle the commotion.

He seems to have everyone's attention,
and it appears that was the intention.
He took a deep breath and looked around the
room, that now felt like a convention.
He seemed cautious, as if he was thinking, "Let
me not screw up this pension."
He said, "There was a bullying incident that
happened, and right now we're focused on
prevention.
Even though everyone involved was punished
and spoken to, we need further comprehension.

Because now others are copying and trying to
do the same to their peers.                    332

Not realizing the damage that was done that will last for years."

Myrtle is there with her eyebrows arched, and it's probably because of the dance.
Wish there was something I could do, wish we had another chance.

I didn't want to go at first, but now we're good friends.
She might be a little weird, but hey, not too long ago, I was wearing Depends.

Hmmm… I see Simone is sitting next to Pretty Boy Shawn.
He's ready to swoop down on her like a pigeon does to bread on the lawn.

If you only knew all the stories of Shawn people tell us.
What is wrong with me, am I really getting jealous?
I had to remind myself, you turned her down the way Hank turns down lettuce,
After she did me wrong at the park in front of the fellas.
I must be "BooBoo The Fool" because to me she's still precious.

I'm imagining her wearing my name around her neck, engraved on a necklace.

Hurst continued, "Many of you don't realize how your actions affect others,
Then you try to hide the hurt with different covers.

Before you do or say something, think of how you'd feel;
Or realize there's something wrong with all of us, is what I want to reveal.
It could be physical or internal, you'll discover this with every layer you peel.
If you don't know what I'm talking about, here is an example to make it more real."

I wonder what Hurst is up to; must be something he found?
He takes off his glasses, while his head is hanging toward the ground.

Slowly picks his head up, with his eyes closed.
When he opens them up, one eye is normal but the other is exposed.

The last thing I suspected was for our

principal to have a lazy eye.
With a solemn tone, he began telling us how he
was teased, and why.

He said, "My first name is William, so back in
school, they called me 'One-Eyed Willy.'
I remembered 'One-Eye Burst Hurst' and other
names that were silly.

When I look down, my left eye is still looking
toward the sky.
I'm legally blind in it, but I still get by.
When I'm driving, to keep from crashing, on the
right one I rely.
It's hard to win an argument when I'm saying
no, and my left eye is asking why.
Public speaking was always defeating, the
excuse I've used was 'I'm too shy!'—
Because I refused to make eye contact, so I
didn't even try.
They told me surgery couldn't fix it; as a kid
that made me cry.

And for a while I wore sunglasses in school,
And even now, my glasses have a little tint in
them to fool.

At one point I was a one-month absentee.

Now, that's how much bullying has affected me!
Anybody else want to share how bullying
affected them, so everyone can see?"

The caf was quiet before, but now you can hear
a pin drop.
Their faces looked like their stomachs and
intestines were twisting into a knot.
It was like everyone was thinking about what
issues they've got—
Which ones they could share, and how many
others they could not.
 Then a hand went up— it was Mr. Dozer ready
to put himself on the spot.
Said, "I don't speak about this much, but I'm
gonna give it a shot."

Smiling while pointing to his head, "This is a hair
piece,  I know it's hard to believe."
The students call me 'Lace front Dozer', 'Tupe
Dozer', and 'Mr. Man-Weave'.

I know kids were just being kids, by ragging on
me with regularity,"
He paused and bit his bottom lip, "but I got lung
cancer, two packs of cigarettes a day was the
recipe;

336

And so, I lost my hair from chemotherapy.

I know the hair piece looks stupid, I'm not naive.
But it's to make me feel better, I'm not trying to deceive.
Don't feel sorry for me, I just want to see every last one of you achieve.
A strong wind has yet to blow my hairpiece away, for that, I am relieved!
The tumor is the size of a softball, you wouldn't believe—
Sometimes it feels like I can't breathe!
I cough up blood every morning, sometimes there's even blood on my sleeve."

That caught us all off guard.
Everyone loves Dozer, but ended up showing him no regard.
But he is still nice to us, others would have been too scarred.
I glanced around the room, and many took this news hard.

"I love being your teacher, I love being alive, I don't ever want to leave.
I should've known better— my dad died from cancer, and it took forever to grieve." 337

Hearing our favorite teacher speak, might have made the room sway.

Then Myrtle stands up and says, "I have something to say."

Before she said anything, there seemed to be some kind of delay.

First she's fiddling with her hands, is she taking her gloves off? No way!

Why is she closing her eyes? Seems like she's starting to pray.

It seems she's trying to convince herself to continue, but part of her won't obey.

She's never taken the gloves off before, but now it's in play.

In the past she figured if they don't know, they can't hurt her, which sounds very cliché.

Her gloves are finally off, then someone accidentally drops a tray.

Her hands were discolored, like a brown and white collage or painting on display.

She seems out of breath, and says, "I've been afraid of the comments, and of this day.

It's a skin disorder called vitiligo, and it's not going away.

Some think I'm a mime; to them, that's what the gloves convey.

There's no way to reverse it, so there were few options I had to weigh.
I tried to get a tan— you know, the kind that you spray.
Even tried to soak them in Clorox; but it didn't work, much to my dismay.
So I figured I'd keep the gloves on, it was a smaller price to pay."
She sits down and crosses her fingers and says "I'm done now, okay."

Wiffersnuv, who I didn't realize was in the corner of the room,
Decided to speak wearing his Coach Hines from Mad TV costume.

He said, "Listen up, Pip Squeaks," like this was the gym,
As if he was still poking the non-athletic kids with his words, like a bobby pin.
"I've been called 'Mr. WifferBalls', 'Scrotum Neck', and 'Testicle Chin'."
He said it's a cyst, so no more making fun of him.

He said "I've tried to wear a turtleneck, but the boob on my throat was glaring.

I can't wear ties because it cuts the circulation, and it starts pulsating and flaring.

So v-necks and mocknecks are the only shirts I'm wearing.

My wife doesn't like to go out to eat no more, since people be staring.

I tried to remove this freaking damn thing, excuse me for swearing,

But in a few months it came back, even more daring."

At this point, I'm no longer caring."

Then Hurst shook his hand and said, "Thank you for sharing."


"Okay! My turn to share!" Out of nowhere we heard Suzie blurt.

She has her back turned to us, but she's not an introvert.

She commences, "I'm not going to lie— I love food— especially dessert.

When they call me fat, or 'Suzie Snacks,' and say I use a bed sheet for a skirt,

It rips me up inside, can't believe how much it hurts.

The guilt becomes too much after I eat a large amount in a spurt."

Her eyes are watery now, as if they're about to squirt...
"Then I go to the bathroom or outside, and force myself to throw up in the dirt.
Because of it, I feel weak often and even fainted at a concert.
I've tried different diets, it gets better, then I revert.
The acid from my stomach is starting to rot my teeth, and it's becoming overt.
Instead of my dad's donuts, more nutrients I need to insert.
To end up in the hospital again, is what I need to avert.
My family is worried about me, they say with death I flirt.
The Doc says I'm sick, I'm bulimic; I feel fine, but he's the expert."
*Now I realize why sometimes I see dried vomit on her shirt.*


I can't be the only one that feels like running away, but no one is moving.
I can't believe what I'm hearing, my conscious is refusing.
*What's that?* I'm two tables away and I can hear Hank chewing.

If I can hear it, the people closest to him
must be thinking, what is he doing?
Sounds like someone stomping on leaves
that've been accruing,
Or crushing soda can after soda can, I'm
assuming.

Pete was knocked out cold during the last
testimony.
I only noticed because it sounded like a tiger
trying to scare a pony.
Man— this dude would probably sleep through
his own graduation ceremony!

Who am I kidding? He has a decent grade in
gym, his one and only.
He's probably dreaming of ways to get back at
his former homie—
They are arch rivals, their friendship was
phony.

Why is Mitch looking at me like he wants me to
step up to the plate?
Does he really think I'm going to stand up and
say I peed in the bed till eight?
I've been humiliated plenty at this school—
yeah, nah, he's going to have to wait.

It's so intense in here, it's overwhelming; from my thoughts I need to separate.

Then I started daydreaming about that time Mitch was teaching me how to punch straight.

Now that I think about it, that time was great. I'm surprised how many bonds he and I had a chance to create.

I still practice at home in front of the mirror, as if the reflection is my inmate.

Then all of a sudden Mitch raised his hand, as if embracing his fate.

He said, "I get clowned for having big eyes, they say my eyes are overweight.

They say from here I can read a street sign from the interstate.

This girl saw a pic of my eyes, then I got stood up when we were supposed to roller skate.

I usually laugh it off, then take my anger out on others; some of you can relate.

I wish none of this happened, I hope I can start with a clean slate."

The whole time his fist is clinched, but I noticed it late.

He said, "What they don't realize— I'm dyslexic— and reading in front of others— I hate.

Some letters and numbers seem backwards to me, in my mind that's how it translates.    343

For a week I didn't eat because I read my lunch card wrong.
Sometimes I get on the wrong bus, or take the wrong train, and end up where I don't belong.

For a long time I thought I was doing well, but I was constantly called a retard.
I kept reading a 60 as 90 on my test papers and report card."

*Oh, man! Mitch too? He could have told me, we could have had a chat.*
What good is a friend, if he ain't got your back?
What's up with Fernando, why is he looking like that?
He looks like a rat that's been cornered by a ferocious cat,
Awaiting to get thrusted in the jaws of combat,
As if his strength is wavering and his courage is flat.

Stick is sitting on the other side, toward Flakes he's peeping.

He's paranoid for no reason, always looking at Flakes saying, "He has the strangest feeling."

Pete finally woke up, there's something on the ground he is punting.
Does he really want to speak, or is he fronting?
Hands on his hips and he's grunting.
Pete can't ever let himself be outdone by Mitch, I guess he has to say something.

He revealed, "I get dissed because my skin looks like this— no one is sympathetic.
They call me 'The Unibrow', and to me it's pathetic.
I'll fall asleep at any moment, even with my eyes open, and it's genetic.
Just in case ya'll didn't know, it's a disorder— I'm narcoleptic.

One time I fell asleep in a tanning booth, and ended up looking like the main course at Red Lobster.
Our house was broken into and I was knocked out cold, in front of the robbers.

I will never be able to drive, because the car becomes a death trap.
One minute I'm cruising and honking at the honeys, the next  I'm taking a nap.

I do push-ups because I can never lift weights.
If I do, in the middle of a set, I'll fall asleep and get crushed by 100-pound plates.

I went roller skating and got a concussion, because I fell asleep and hit my head.
I need help; if I'm not careful, I could end up dead.
But some rather put a pizza box on my head and pepperonis on my pimples, while I'm sleeping instead."

Pete and Mitch speaking must have started a chain reaction.
Because Hank decided to take a break from eating, his only passion.

First he banged on the table and said, "What the hell!"
Started scratching his arms, as if trying to peel off a shell.

"I've been called 'Butt-crack Breath', and told
that I'm shaped like I swallowed the Liberty
Bell.
Never told anyone about my thyroid disease—
that affects my glands and hormones, as well.
I've tried to go on diets, but end up eating
the menu after my appetite begins to swell."
He gave a scowl then turned around, like
there's someone he's trying to repel
And says, "Don't think I didn't notice no one
ever sits next to me, I can tell."
*Dang, so that must be why he overeats and why
he always has a smell!*
"Supposedly, I leave a scent behind that got
me banned from another hotel.
I have to use a special deodorant, which very
few places sell.
When I bathe, it's hard to lift and get in
every crevice with the shower gel.
I wish I didn't have to wear a three-piece suit
when in the pool, but that's what 'Man Boobs'
will compel.
And I don't appreciate getting shoved in a
garbage can, but on that— I won't dwell."

Fernando's now biting his nails, he must be real bothered;
The way he's nibbling them, it's like by corn on the cob he's sponsored.
It's as if he's screaming, but it's a scream that's not heard.
As if by fear, or some unknown anxiety, he's being conquered.

Sam quickly got up, "I've heard all the jokes. My head makes a blimp look mini.
They call me 'Drip Drip', 'Head Master Flex', 'Big Head Smalls' and for short, 'Biggie.'
And I couldn't be a Santa Helper, because my head would get stuck in the chimney.
The reason why I'm always in the bathroom— well it's because I have only one kidney."

The memory of what we did to Sam in the bathroom, now has my mind to haunt.
Sam is rocking back and forth, as if with insanity he flaunts.
He said, "I didn't mean to take things out on Fernando, I'm not mad at him, I'm mad at his aunt.
And seeing him everyday in school, just feels like a taunt."

And for a minute, the look on everyone's face was pure confusion.
I'm going from scenario to scenario, trying to draw conclusions.

Why would he be mad at Flake's aunt? Did she not let him pee?
She's not the woman that Sam's mom left his father for, or is she?

Mrs. Vanswoon walked to the middle of the caf, next to Hurst.
Is she going to speak, or let it build to an outburst?
She put her hand to her face, as if she needed a nurse.
She had the most sudden, saddest look in her eyes, as if she's been cursed.

She began with, "I'm 'Witch Vanswoon'; or 'Two Face' is another name I go by."
Oh no! She must've heard everything, she could probably hear a mosquito cry!
She said, "Six months ago, my husband left me and I was traumatized.
The shock led to a stroke, and the left side of my face became paralyzed.

349

Some of the comments I heard felt like I
was being terrorized.
I would look in the mirror and ask, what did I
do to be this penalized?
Thought I was a good wife, good mother and
good teacher, but I've been demoralized.
I sent my son to go live with his dad; I
thought by my face he'd be terrified.
Sometimes I lock the door to the classroom,
sit in the dark completely mesmerized.
When I go to the grocery store, I pray to
God I'm not recognized."

As I looked around the room, so many faces
were ashamed.
Others looking uncomfortable, probably
wishing they never came.
I never called her 'Two Face', but for 'Witch
Vanswoon', I shared the blame.
I can see Vanswoon's hands shaking, while
adjusting her eyeglass frame.

Then before I knew it, Carl spoke,
And Mr. Wannabe, stand-up comedian
started with a joke.
Guess he's trying to disrupt this somber
mood, thick enough to make you choke.

He conceded, "If you're wondering, yes, this
is my real nose, it ain't broke.
I was told I looked like a white chocolate
chip cookie, cause with moles my back is
cloaked."
He put on a fake smile and his eyes were
misty, like the air was filled with smoke.
Admittedly, he continues, "But it's the worst
hearing kids make fun of my mom after
having a stroke. "

Before anyone could even begin to process
what Carl just implied,
Hurst circled back to his purpose to shed
light on where this moment would reside.

He said, "You see that— that's exactly what
I mean!
There's something wrong with all of us; no
one's perfect, we're all in between.

We all have said or done something, without
knowing the whole truth.
Be careful what you say or do, have a little
couth.
You never fully know what someone's going
through, and this right here was proof."

Then Flakes finally stands up, without making a sound.
But he's hesitating, like he's contemplating on sitting back down.

His bottom lip is quivering, as if electricity is passing through it.
His voice is crackling and breaking; whatever he's trying to say, he's struggling to do it.

Is he admitting he has psoriasis or dandruff, is that what he's trying to say?
Is he trying to tell us why he's always hiding in the hallway?
Is he trying to tell us he's Puerto Rican, not Dominican— is that what he's trying to convey?
Is he trying to tell us why Sam doesn't like his aunt? Well then, okay.
So many questions, my thoughts in disarray.
He asserted, "I'm tired of you all questioning what I am, the answer is... I'm gay."
And not even two seconds after he said it, he ran away.

# RECONCILIATION

## Chapter 22

Since the principal's cafeteria meeting last week,
There's been a different mood amongst students and school staff I'm seeing.
A sense of cautiousness, as if no one knows when to laugh, and I haven't noticed any teasing.
It seems we look at our teachers in a new light, and it's gleaming.
We all seem to have a better understanding of one another, and how we're dealing.
Between teachers and students alike, understanding is breeding.
Can't believe that was the secret Fernando was stressed about revealing.
I wonder if that's what Stanley was referring to when he said, "I have the strangest feeling."

Now we're willing to share with one another.
I still can't believe Mrs. Vanswoon is Carl's mother.

There is a fond sense of respect for the courage we all have shown.
As I walk around, I notice many are speaking in an empathetic tone.

The vibe is so different, don't know how long it will last;
Regardless, we've all learned more than anyone can ask.

We've been introduced to strategies that will supposedly stop bullying activity.
I've seen that addressing aggressive behavior with negative responses leads to more negativity.
Now I believe we all have to be more thoughtful with our words and actions, and increase our sensitivity.
I've realized everyone is going through something, even though we don't know the specificity.
I learned what bullying is, and what bullying isn't— and its toxicity.
I understand what snitching is, what it isn't, its intentions and delivery.
We engaged in various forms of restorative practices, to foster community.

I can see now there are bullies everywhere
and everyone has the ability.
I was educated on why people bully, and it
gave me much clarity.
I realized it has nothing to do with me, and
that's the reality...
And to not take it personal, has to become
my mentality.


It's a Friday morning and after class, Mitch
and I spoke.
He said we should go to the mall and hang,
and I thought it was a joke.
I hardly ever go to the mall; Mama always
says, "We're broke."
She'll look at the price tags and almost croak.
If I ask Mama for anything, she'll say, "Oh,
you think it's crack I smoke?"
Do I look like I just got off the boat?" Then
she cautions with, "Nope!
"It's expensive! Do I look like a drug dealer?
Do I look like I sell dope?
You need to pray on it, and I'm not Jesus or
the Pope!"
Most of the clothes we get are from the flea
market, that's why my sense of style has no
hope.

If it's not from the flea market, then it's a
hand-me-down.
Oh, and if you don't know what a hand-me-
down is, let me explain to you this noun.
Wearing your older brother's old clothes when
the blacks are grey and the beige used to be
brown...
That's a hand-me-down!
If you have old clothes or shoes from a cousin
or family member, and in them you drown—
That's a hand-me-down.
If you have clothes from the thrift shop in
your town—
That's a hand-me-down.
Clothes from the Salvation Army with those
yellow tags throughout the compound—
Are also hand-me-downs.
Wearing your sister's unisex t-shirt that she
used to wear as a night gown—
That's a hand-me-down.
I told Mitch, "I have to ask my mom if I can
go, but I like how that sounds."

At that moment, Mr. Charles walks up to me
and he is excited.
He looks as if a unicorn was just sighted.

His spit almost landed on my eyebrow, while through the air it glided.
He said, "I spoke to Dozer and Vanswoon about how the group was indicted.
Myrtle being hurt and excluded from the dance has us upset and united.
We thought the punishments were harsh, but with the principal we're still sided.
You're both good kids, and Myrtle has the highest grades in school," he highlighted.
"During lunch, we will prepare Dozer's room; decorations and music will be provided.
It will be a surprise dance for Myrtle, and you're both invited!
And Daniel, we'll need you to get her, but tell her nothing...nothing," he recited.
"It's only for 20 minutes, but I'm sure she'll be delighted."

That's pretty cool for them to do that for us...
She's on the Debate Team, Honor Roll, Principal's List, Orchestra, and Chorus.

She's everybody's favorite student, I get it.
We wouldn't have been able to get back at these bullies without her; I give her credit.

And even before that, she always stood up for me.
She's been a good friend; can't wait to see how happy she's going to be.


At the end of fourth period on the way to the caf walking slow
Stanley and I happened to run into Fernando.
Stanley called him over and he usually doesn't do so;
Says, "Hey Fernando, sit with us during lunch, bro."
Fernando was like, "You guys won't be uncomfortable from what I said a week ago?
All of the boys stayed away from me this week, the way Hank stays away from cardio.
But the girls stayed status quo, and just went with the flow.
All I ever heard from the boys is 'that's gay' and sometimes 'no homo'.
That's why I rarely ever spoke; they even said it was gay when I said 'hello'.
I was afraid of how my friends' real feelings would show.
Felt like I betrayed some people, but I was betraying my ability to grow.

I questioned my decision, but I didn't want to keep putting on a show.
I was confused because I kept seeing signs of coming out, everywhere I go."
Stick was like, "Nah, we're cool; you're our friend, sit with us, please don't say no.
It's just that sometimes you look at me in a weird way." Then Fernando said, "Oh!"
 "Besides, my brother is gay, we found out before he got locked up, you know."

Once we got to the caf, I couldn't eat slow as a turtle,
Because in 20 minutes, I would have to go find Myrtle.

At this point, Suzie went over to Hank, who's sitting next to the trash.
Heard them speaking about overeating and having a food stash,
And how they like Doritos, burritos and prefer potatoes mashed.
Spoke about which diets work, and how it hurts to have extra fat on the calf.
Suzie said, "You're having a crack attack. Pull your pants up, don't you feel the draft?"
Mitch's former buddies kept their distance, spread out like a rash.

Tim, Pete and Hank seem to still be on the not-speaking path;
Sam was the only one not in the caf.
Mitch went to sit and explain to each one the cause of the clash.
Said it was him who was spreading their business and said, "Just do the math.
Don't be mad at each other, direct it towards me— the wrath.

I'm the only one who knew enough secrets to pass.
I'm sorry for what I did, I would like us to be friends, like we were in the past."
I'm not sure if their problems were hashed.
My 20 minutes are almost up, and soon I must dash.

The very next moment, Matt pulled up with something to share.
He said, "There's something strange with Instagram and Snapchat that we're unaware."
Everyone quickly grabbed their phones to check their social media with cautious despair.
"What? Look! I have 10,000 new followers!" Tim declared.
Then Pete affirmed, "Oh snap, me too," and Mitch was like, "Show me, where?"

Hank put the food down and placed his phone next to Tim's and Pete's to compare.
Soon after he said, "I guess I do, too." But no one else said they saw a change, which is rare.
Mitch just sat there with disappointment after a long, hard stare.
Him and I had notifications and follower requests that were still bare.
Must be something wrong with the apps that someone needs to repair.
And why only those three? I sense something fishy is in the air.
Did Matt hack their pages again, but this time with a flair?—
Perhaps to appease the guilt most of us felt and make things fair;
But all he said was, "I had nothing to do with it, I swear!"


I quickly left Stanley and Fernando there talking about the lousy cafeteria french fries.
Myrtle doesn't have lunch this period, she must have band, I surmise.
Once I got to the band room, 'she went to the bathroom', is what the band teacher implies.
I figured I'd wait; but after 10 minutes she still didn't show, maybe someone was told lies.

She must have fell in the toilet, inadvertently capsized.

Maybe she's having a secret ceremony, and with toilet water she's being baptized.

Went to Dozer's room to let him know I'm waiting for her, while my patience dries.

He told me the period would be over soon, to go find her, and try to improvise.

Went back to the band room, but she was still not back with the guys.

Figured I go wait by the girls bathroom for her, because I thought it was wise.

As I hit the staircase to get there, I exhaled in sighs.

I'm also out of shape, I have forearms for thighs.

I hear a voice behind the staircase that I recognize—

Now I'm creeping towards it, like I'm part of a covert operation of Super Geek Spies.

I found Myrtle, but instead of surprising her, I was the one surprised—

Because guess who was back there with her— I can't believe my eyes!

Did I interrupt something? Is it nothing? In the face of denial, the truth flies.

It feels like this is a moment when part of me dies,

Or when the executioner in his black hearse
finally arrives—
It's Myrtle and Sam kissing like a scene from
Days Of Our Lives!

I went back to the caf, but with only 10
minutes left, I probably shouldn't.
I should've went back and told Dozer what
happened... but I couldn't.

I owe it to them, after all their planning and
consideration— to let them know.
But not right now, maybe later though.
Saying to myself, "Don't let it bother you, it's
not like she's your girlfriend, bro."
It still feels like betrayal, or some type of
ego blow.

I go sit next to Stanley and Fernando, now
Mitch is at our table, too.
They're laughing at some epic fails from
Mitch's phone, one with an animal and a man
at the zoo.

Out of nowhere, Hank drops to the floor
sitting two tables down.
Everyone quickly jumps up and crowds around.

*What did I miss?* Wish this was a DVD I could have rewound.

A clear sight of Hank at this point can't be found.

Should I climb on the back of others, as if it's a mound.

Did he attempt to go toe-to-toe with the Grim Reaper for another round?

How serious is it? Is he nurse's office or hospital-bound?

I think someone is yelling for help, but in chaos and confusion it's drowned.

Mitch carved a path as usual, and for that he's renowned.

And we caught a glimpse of Hank's hands around his throat, while laying on the ground.

His eyes and mouth are open wide, tongue dangling, while making a gagging sound.

The lunch lady tries to clear the way to see what's happening.

The look on her face was as if the worst she's imagining.

Suzie said, "He's choking, help me get him up!"
They tried to lift Hank, but it looked like they were backing up a dump truck.

It was hard for her to put her arms around
his gut.

Ok, they finally did, then Suzie performed
the Heimlich maneuver,
At the same time trying to avoid that he
smelled like manure.

She gave one thrust, nothing happened; now
it's not looking promising.
Another thrust, and he's choking even more,
almost as if he's vomiting.

She did a third thrust and now Hank is almost
purple, like the late Prince's coat.
With the fourth thrust, Suzie looks ready to
quit, it's about to be 'all she wrote.'
But then a piece of broccoli— out of nowhere
— flew out of his throat!

Then before we knew it, the school nurse,
Mr. Charles and Hurst were already there.
Five minutes later, you heard an ambulance's
siren coming from somewhere.

While the nurse is checking on Hank, I'm over
here getting my thoughts together.

365

Out of all the bad things Hank has eaten, it's a piece of broccoli that almost buries him forever?

And out of all the people who could've saved him, who does? Miss Vomit Stain on her sweater.

While he's being placed on a gurney, Suzie grabs his hand and applies some mild pressure.

She says, "Don't worry Hank, when you get out the hospital, we'll get healthy. He responds with, "We better."


The bell finally rings and everyone heads to their next class.

While walking, who pulls up next to me?

Without her big butt friend, with all the sass—

Simone! I noticed by no dudes she's being harassed,

Based on her angelic reflection from the display case's glass.

She says, "Can you believe what just happened?"

My response was, "You saw Myrtle and Sam, too? I never imagined."

She was like, "What are you talking about?" My face she examined.

"I'm referring to Hank choking, laying on the ground while his throat fastened."

*Oh, no! Did my leaky lips just put me in a jam?*
Sometimes I wish my jaw could stay shut like a clam.
Then she looked at me and said, "What happened to Myrtle and Sam?"
*Should I answer the question, or play dumb as a lamb?*
For a second, I thought I had what it takes to not give in to this angel, but it's all a sham.
So I said, "I saw them kissing!"— And Simone said, "Damn!"
"She's just a friend, so I shouldn't be mad, but I am.
They were in the back of the staircase; before they could see me, I ran."
She said, "What did you expect? She did it because she can."
I made a few inferences, and whatever she meant by that, I had to scan.
She explained, "Sam and Myrtle used to like each other for about a six-week span."
And those words hit me like a rained-out concert to a disappointed fan;

And my head began throbbing like that one time
Mama smacked me with the frying pan.
"Are you serious?! I turned *you* down, because
to go to the dance with *her* was the plan!"
*Did she only ask me to the dance to make Sam
jealous? Oh, man!*
Someone should've gave me a warning before
this whole 'ask me to the dance' thing began.
But instead, my better judgement was
kidnapped and driven off in a van.
This is so embarrassing; I'm about to hide my
face behind a paper fan.

I took my right fist, and against my thigh it
slammed,
After I realized how badly I just got scammed!

She said, "I guess you're free to go with
whoever you want, now."
I said, "No, me going to any school activity,
they won't allow."

Did you ever find a date?" The answer to that
question had me stuck like a blood clot.
She said she did and looked away as she did her
'Miss America' trot."
She said, "I'm going with Shawn, I almost
forgot." 368

*Does she mean Pretty Boy Shawn?* All of a sudden, I felt 130 degrees hot.

Felt like a hot dog or corn on the cob, boiling in a pot.

Even though I can't go, I felt the courage inside me rot.

Out of all the boys, really? Shawn had to fill that spot?

Saying to myself, *"Come on Daniel, you think you're going to stop liking her? You're not!*
*Take a chance and shoot your shot!*
*Even though compared to Shawn, I'm orangutan snot.*
*But this might be the last chance you've got!"*

*But what am I saying? Am I asking for her number or a date?*
*Am I asking to walk her to class or walk her home, but wait…*

*Mama won't let me use the phone; if she says yes, she'll go disconnect the whole console.*

The next words out of my mouth are…"Do you bowl?

Maybe if you give me your phone number, I can call me, and we can all go bowling."

*OMG, that didn't come out right.* Someone passed by and is laughing and rolling.

She was like, "You want my phone number to call yourself?" My nervous 'Super Geek' game just wasn't flowing.

*What am I thinking? Who's we? Would Mama and Pops be chaperoning?*

Now there's an awkward silence— will she say yes? It's killing me not knowing.

I'm tapping my feet; for a less than embarrassing outcome, I'm hoping.

Every second that passes, I sense the fear inside me growing.

Then she went in her book bag— it looks like a stall tactic is approaching.

She's looking for something, maybe it's pepper spray, or a nice way to say 'no way' is unfolding.

But instead, it's a pen she's holding.

Wrote her number on a piece of paper, no joking.

And like a winning lottery ticket in my pocket it's going.


Later on that night when Mama came home, I asked if I could meet Mitch at the mall, with the most polite tone.

She said, "You don't need anything at the mall, I just bought you new sneakers."
She put the box in front of me, and for the first time they were keepers!

I never like any sneakers or shoes she picks.
She usually gets me knock-offs, or no-frills kicks.
Normally my Nike would say Sike, and my Vans would say Vics;
Or the Nike check mark would be upside down or backwards, nothing that could be fixed.
But this time, they looked official! Guess the flea market stepped up their tricks.
I begged Mama if I could wear them to the mall to meet Mitch;
She finally caved in, as if I were an annoying itch.

When I get to the mall, I'm sitting waiting for Mitch— and I began thinking…
Everyone has a story; I know a little of Mitch's from all the times we were linking.
*How did everyone get like this? I don't even have an inkling.*
*How long has Hank been stinking???*

*So Pete has been falling asleep like this his whole life???*
*Is it just a rumor? What **really** happened with Sam's dad and his wife?*

*If Vanswoon is Carl's mother, how come he never responded to the things he heard?*
*How is Suzie the queen of gossip, but gets treated like a nerd?*
*Did Matt hack their accounts again? How were 10,000 followers transferred?*
*Has Fernando always been like this? Maybe something more occurred.*
*Were these bullies always bullies— was something inside them triggered?*
*Why did Myrtle deceive me, was the truth ever considered?*

Then, suddenly I hear comments and some laughter...
"He has on Yikes," and, "those are fake" was part of the chatter.
They even called them Double N's for 'Not Nike', and that got me even madder.
The voices are getting closer, make no mistake, I'm about to scatter.
*Here we go with this bullying thing again, another unwanted chapter.*

*These fake sneakers got me served up on a platter.*

*I'm dying to escape— someone please, drop me a ladder!*

*I have a decision to make, and have to avoid another disaster.*

*According to Hurst, I got a couple of choices to factor-*

*If I laugh and walk away, will that matter?*

*Do I give them a blank stare? Not react at all, even though I'm really not a good actor.*

*Do I add to the jokes? I might crack jokes in my head, but this one requires more practice to master.*

*Or just get up and tell them how funny they are; just flatter?*

I felt like I was a pitcher trying to figure which pitch to throw to the batter.

Which one can I actually execute, one of the first three, or the latter?

I gotta commit to one, or I'll make things worse after.

Saying to myself— *remember, they're not attacking you, they're attacking what you represent, rather.*

After everything we all have gone through, why can't people stop it?!

What am I gonna do? I've got to hurry... OK. I've got it!               373

# Prologue To Mitch's Story

Hey Daniel,

We were supposed to meet at the mall at three, but the time is almost four.
I wasn't trying to stand you up and ruin our rapport,
But my lazy dad made me late; always sending me on errands, after I'm done with each chore.
This time he sent me to buy cigarettes to go with the bottle he brought back from the liquor store.

The graffiti on this train I can't read, it might as well be in Latin.
The train is packed as usual, between two people I'm flattened.
Even though she's old as hell, the lady to my left-skin feels like satin.
If it's a thing to smell like a ton of cheap cologne, the man to my right must be the captain.
Oh my God,  I think I took the wrong train— this ain't Grand Central Station in Manhattan!

375

Am I really doing this? It's not too late to turn back, and pretend I forgot my sweater.
I only have 15 dollars, maybe I should go back and get more cheddar.
My friendships and school have finally taken a turn for the better,
But I'd rather be homeless and have no return address for this letter.
Don't know where I'm going to end up, but we can't be under the same roof together.
If he thinks I'm going to tell people that white stuff under the mattress is mine—
NEVER!

He wasn't always like this, he wasn't always this bad.
I told you what happened to my mom, but I never said what happened to my dad.

When I got back with the cigarettes, he kept yelling; I'm sure the neighbors heard the roar.
I snatched his vodka, and down the sink I began to pour;
Then he grabbed my neck and threw me on the floor.
And so I lost it, and kicked him till my legs got sore.
While he was on the ground, I stomped on him like I was marching in the Marine Corps.

He tried to grab on to me, but instead my shirt he tore.
Then ran away before he could pull out the belt from the top drawer—
Threw at him a dusty old vase from our junkyard decor.
Before I left the house, I told him he's a drunk, and won't see me no more.
As I left, I heard him say, "That's why your Mama's a whore!"
I still remember how it all began, this father and son war.
My phone is ringing— it's him— what's he calling for?
It's still ringing-should I put it on silent? It's getting harder to ignore.
He left a message— should I listen to it, and right after delete it? This I swore.
He asked me, if I called ACS, because they're here with the police standing behind the door.
I don't want nothing to do with him, but him getting locked up— I never saw.
Heard him yelling at them, saying disciplining his kid ain't against the law.
And he won't open— for the police to come get him-I'm on the other end of the phone in awe!
Then all of a sudden there was a loud bang, and a scream out of some woman's jaw.
Did they shoot him? Not sure, the message ended premature.

How I'm feeling right now is confusing, and
too much to endure.
That's it for now, someone is watching; I
gotta be more obscure.

Mitch

P.S. I'll write again, when I know for sure
what happened.
I had to run away; I could've ended up dead
if I hadn't.

# Acknowledgments

First and foremost, I'm grateful to God for providing me with the ability and the tribulations that led to this path. I'm grateful for my beautiful wife, who not only is the backbone of my dreams, but a loving partner who worked tirelessly on editing this novel. I'm grateful for my 12-year-old son Jordan, who when he was 8 years old, provided the motivation for this novel. I'm grateful for my oldest daughter Zoï, for always giving her teenage insight to making the novel incredibly impressionable. I'm grateful for my youngest children, Justin and Alexia, for forcing me to have the energy to work as hard as I can, and for as long as I can. I'm grateful to my parents and sister for all of their disguised blessings. Thank you- Paul Jean, for sparking the ideas that led to this project. Thank you- Beniel Santiago, for your collaboration in illustrating such wonderful characters. Thank you— Alex Acevedo, for all of your creative assistance in bringing the characters to life. Thank you— Robert Dennis, for your assistance in making sure every chapter was just as good as the last.

# Meet the Author

Antoine G. Larosiliere is a Haitian immigrant who is married with four beautiful children. His wife is an educator, and he himself has been teaching for over 15 years. Antoine currently teaches in the Bronx, where humor is a huge component of his teaching methods. He also created an anti-bullying program named, *Empowering Communities Against Bullying* (ECAB), which was another major inspiration for this novel.

Made in the USA
Lexington, KY
28 October 2019